APR 1 0 2007

POLICIES AND PROCEDURES TO PREVENT FRAUD AND EMBEZZLEMENT

POLICIES AND PROCEDURES

TO PREVENT FRAUD AND EMBEZZLEMENT

GUIDANCE, INTERNAL CONTROLS, AND INVESTIGATION

EDWARD J. McMILLAN, CPA, CAE

WILEY

John Wiley & Sons. Inc.

For general information on our other products and services, or technical support, please contact our Customer Care Department within the United States at 800-762-2974, outside the United States at 317-572-3993 or fax 317-572-4002.

Wiley also publishes its books in a variety of electronic formats. Some content that appears in print may not be available in electronic books.

For more information about Wiley products, visit our Web site at http://www.wiley.com.

Library of Congress Cataloging-in-Publication Data

McMillan, Edward J., 1949-
    Policies & procedures to prevent fraud and embezzlement: guidance, internal controls, and investigation / Edward J. McMillan.
        p. cm.
    Includes index.
    Contents: Embezzlement: who does it and when — Statement of auditing standart no. 99, consideration of fraud in a financial statement audit" — Essential internal control and administrative procedures to avoid embezzlement — Clever examples of embezzlement — Steps to take if you have been victimized by fraud! — Identity theft — Internal control analysis, documentation, and recommendations for improvement.
    ISBN-13: 978-0-471-79003-7 (pbk.)
    ISBN-10: 0-471-79003-6 (pbk.)
    1. Auditing, Internal. 2. Fraud—Prevention. 3. Embezzlement—Prevention. 4. Small business—Management. I. Title.

HF5668.25.M432 2006
658.4'73—dc22

                                                                                            2005046646

Printed in the United States of America

10 9 8 7 6 5 4 3 2 1

Contents

About the Author

Edward J. McMillan, CPA, CAE, is an experienced fraud examiner and teaches fraud prevention courses to organizations such as the American Institute of CPAs, the Maryland Association of CPAs, other state societies of CPAs, the U.S. Chamber of Commerce, and the American Bar Association, among others. Ed also speaks regularly on the subject of fraud prevention at business conventions of all types and can be reached at (410)893-2308 or contacted via email at EMCMILLAN@ SPRINTMAIL.COM.

Acknowledgments

The publisher and author would like to extend gratitude to the following organizations for their generous permission to reprint their copyrighted materials in the body and glossary of this manual:

The American Chamber of Commerce Executives
Fraud and Embezzlement in Small Business:
How It Happens, How You Can Prevent It

Association of Certified Fraud Examiners
Glossary

Preface

Unfortunately, embezzlement and fraud are a reality that all organizations are confronted with.

This manual is designed to help auditing CPAs, internal auditors, fraud investigators, and management understand how to thoroughly evaluate the system of internal controls, expose weaknesses that could lead to fraud, and take corrective action to reduce the possibility of victimization.

Obviously this book cannot guarantee that fraud or embezzlement will be eliminated. However, if the suggestions offered in this manual are implemented, this risk will be reduced substantially.

Disclaimer

The contents of this book should not be construed as legal advice, and in that respect the publisher and author assume no liability or responsibility accordingly. Before implementation, the internal controls, policies, and forms suggested in this book should be reviewed by a competent attorney to ensure compliance with federal, state, and local laws.

Implementing the internal controls, forms, and processes in this book will by no means guarantee that an organization will be protected from fraud. While this book may help to decrease the *possibility* of embezzlement, it is imperative to remain diligent in business practices.

Remember, desperate people resort to desperate action, and where there is a will, there is a way.

About the Companion Website

The sample policies and procedures found in Section Seven of this book are also available in MS-Word format on a Web site designed to accompany this book:

www.wiley.com/go/mcmillan/business_fraud

They can be copies and customized to fit the specific needs of your organization.

Editor's Note: The author has also written a similar book (Wiley 2006) on the subject of fraud prevention policies and procedures designed for the nonprofit community entitled:

Preventing Fraud in Nonprofit Organizations

Embezzlement: Who Does It and When

The Perpetrators: Who They Are, Why They Do It, and How They Are Caught

IN THE REAL WORLD of embezzlement, the perpetrators rarely fit the stereotypical image of someone capable of concocting and carrying out fraud schemes. Rather, they are almost always someone *above suspicion!* The stories of internal theft being carried out by the innocent-appearing young man who sings in the choir or the older woman whom you can count on to remember everyone's birthday are actually the norm. Embezzlers are of any age, sex, race, religion, and income bracket.

Why? Despite the appearance of honesty, you can never be sure of what is going on in someone's personal life, and desperate people are capable of taking desperate action. For example, it is probable that you have no idea that a fellow employee may:

➤ Have a gambling issue
➤ Have an alcohol problem
➤ Have a substance abuse situation
➤ Be experiencing financial difficulties
➤ Have expensive medical bills
➤ Or—enjoy living life on the edge!

There are, however, a few profiles that warrant the attention of management:

Who They Are, Why They Do It

The Disgruntled Employee   Employees who have been passed over for promotion, demoted, reprimanded, or been the subject of disciplinary action often feel they have a justifiable grievance against the organization. People in this situation often feel they have nothing to lose if they are caught in wrongdoing. Additionally, they often rationalize their actions and feel they are justifiably righting a perceived wrong, and they convince themselves they have done nothing wrong.

The Stressed-Out Employee   People experiencing a personal crisis such as a divorce, serious illness, or death in the family often become desperate. It is worth repeating that desperate people often take desperate actions.

Employees Living above Their Means   Employees living an extravagant lifestyle well above their income level are always suspicious. Money needed to fund this lifestyle had to come from somewhere!

The Employee Who Never Takes a Vacation   It is unnatural and unhealthy for people never to take time off. Unfortunately, the reason for this behavior is often that they can't risk having someone else sit at their desk, look at their mail, or answer their telephone because they are hiding something.

Employees Who Are Unnaturally Compulsive about Their Job Responsibilities
As in the case of the employee who never takes a vacation, employees who refuse to share their work with anyone, hide their work, or take work home could also be covering something.

Employees Experiencing Financial Difficulties   People who can't meet their debts and are stretched too thin financially are always of concern. When this situation comes up, consider helping the individual by providing personal financial counseling.

Unfortunately, people sometimes find themselves in dire circumstances. Often this occurs through no fault of their own. There may be health issues, financial difficulties, layoffs, or elderly parents needing assistance. Always remember that desperate people will take desperate action.

Note: Occasionally check where people cash their paychecks. A bank or credit union is the typical place. If an employee owes money, you may see an endorsement over to a private citizen. You may even see checks cashed at liquor stores, pool halls, bars, or other odd places. Or an employee may be using an expensive check-cashing service. Be alert. This may indicate an employee with problems. So a simple review of paycheck endorsements is imperative.

Employees Who Have Drug Problems   People who become addicted to drugs will do almost anything to support their habit, obviously including stealing from their employer. The best way to approach this is to suggest counseling. This type of person should never, of course, be put in a position handling money, checks, and so forth.

The Employee with a Gambling Problem   Most gamblers, of course, are responsible individuals, but people with a gambling problem, particularly illegal gambling through bookies, are a real danger. These people "borrow" money to place bets and intend to repay the "loan" with their winnings, which of course rarely happens. When these people get in over their heads, particularly with the criminal element, they find themselves in a desperate situation and, once again, desperate people will resort to desperate actions.

The Fraud Triangle

To preview the Fraud Triangle noted in "Statement of Auditing Standard No. 99", Section 2 of this handbook:

Incentive: The scenarios described above are examples of the "Incentive," the starting point for fraud.

Opportunity: Too much trust, poor internal controls, lack of supervision by supervisors, no financial audit by independent CPAs, and the like, all create opportunity for fraud. The basic purpose of effective internal controls is to remove the opportunity for fraud.

Rationalization: After a period of time, the perpetrator actually convinces themselves that they are not stealing, but rather self-correcting a perceived wrong such as a pay discrepancy or the like.

How They Get Caught

Just as profiles of embezzlers surprise people, so does uncovering fraud.

Despite belief to the contrary, *most fraud is discovered by accident and due to unanticipated work interruptions,* and not during the course of a CPA's financial audit!

Here is how fraud is uncovered:

➤ During the course of a CPA's financial audit: 2%
➤ As the result of an internal audit: 18%
➤ By whistleblowers: 30%
➤ By pure luck: 50%

Let's break down each category:

CPA Financial Audit   Despite belief to the contrary, it is actually unusual for an audit to uncover an embezzlement. Why? The perpetrator knows what the auditor does and does not look at, as well as what management does and does not look at. This combination, coupled with a weakness in internal controls, is the basis for the important "opportunity" portion of the Fraud Triangle. It is also important to reinforce the fact that auditors are not there to uncover fraud during the course of their audit, but rather to issue an opinion on whether or not the figures in the financial statement are presented fairly, even considering the provisions of SAS 99.

Internal Audits   As you can see, the probability of uncovering fraud rises from just 2% due to a CPA's audit to 18% for an internal audit.

A good internal audit program is very effective if the procedures are followed during the period between the time that the auditors conclude field work for year 1 and return to start field work for year 2. See "The Embezzler's 'Window of Opportunity,'" later in this chapter.

Whistleblowers   The probability of fraud being detected rises to an impressive 30% due to whistleblowers.

It is important to have a whistleblower program coupled with a whistleblower retaliation prohibition policy as part of any organization's administrative policies. These policies are actually a requirement of organizations subject to the Sarbanes-Oxley Act of 2002, but all organizations should give this serious consideration. (See "Whistleblowers," in Section 3 of this handbook.)

Luck   Luck accounts for a whopping 50% of all reported fraud! That is correct— simply stumbling onto something or the thief's carelessness accounts for a full one-half of reported fraud!

The Finance Department

It's unfortunate, but it's a fact—*most* internal embezzlement schemes involve someone assigned to the accounting function. With that in mind, pay particular attention and be diligent when assessing a system of internal controls.

Think about some of the responsibilities individuals have in the typical accounting area:

➤ They receive the organization's checks and cash.
➤ They prepare the bank deposits.
➤ They take the deposits to the bank.
➤ They order checks.
➤ They prepare checks.
➤ They mail checks.
➤ They receive the bank statements.

➤ They prepare payroll.

➤ They prepare payroll tax deposits.

➤ They do the bank reconciliations.

➤ They prepare the financial statements.

➤ They prepare journal entries.

➤ They are the petty cash custodians.

➤ They prepare payroll tax returns.

➤ They have access to the safe.

➤ They activate loans and lines of credit.

➤ They are the sole custodians of the accounting records.

➤ They coordinate and arrange for payment for organization credit card transactions.

➤ They process credit card information from customers.

➤ They prepare W-2s and 1099s.

➤ They process credit card transactions for customers.

➤ They are the custodians of fixed asset records.

➤ They are the custodians of inventory records.

➤ They ultimately write off bad debts from accounts receivable.

➤ They record debt service transactions.

➤ They account for noncash expense such as depreciation and amortization.

Without effective internal controls, any of these responsibilities, in the hands of the wrong individual, could lead to a serious problem. This problem is compounded if the person the accountant reports to is not an accountant also.

When Do They Do It?   In addition to the fact that embezzlers are often above suspicion, many fraud schemes have another similarity. The time of the embezzlement is very likely the same from case to case.

And, exactly, when is that? It's always during a very large "window of opportunity." And that window is most likely to be open *between the time the CPA has left the office after concluding the audit field work for the current year, and the time he or she is scheduled to come back to start the audit for the subsequent year.*

The window of opportunity is the time that the organization has to be the most vigilant. A smart thief is not going to pursue an embezzlement scam when the auditors are on-site or due to come in. In fact, this is the time when the thief will be squeaky clean.

The Embezzler's "Window of Opportunity"

Any accountant experienced in the area of fraud investigation or forensic accounting will emphasize the vital importance of taking thorough and copious notes of every important detail relating to the investigation. Why? Notes will be extremely important in the event that the matter goes to litigation, because it may be *years* before the matter goes to trial. Obviously, people move on to other firms, people retire, and there is an understandable memory lapse over time. If good notes are taken, others can proceed because detailed information is available.

Over time, an experienced fraud examiner will notice that similarities often exist when comparing the details of various fraud scenarios. Although this is certainly not an absolute, the vast majority of embezzlement schemes share the following:

> ➤ Weak internal controls
> ➤ Too much trust
> ➤ Poor management oversight
> ➤ Lack of a financial audit
> ➤ No background checks on key positions
> ➤ Lack of independent checks on bank statements and credit card statements
> ➤ Failure to take advantage of the bank's Positive Pay service
> ➤ Failure to take advantage of the bank's Lockbox service

Another striking consistency that has surfaced over time is *when* most of the embezzlements addressed in this book occurred, and this is *between the time the auditors conclude their field work for one year and return to start their field work for the subsequent year.* Obviously, the perpetrators of a scam, regardless of how clever, will in all likelihood put the fraudulent activity on hold while the auditors are physically in the office, as they want to give the impression to the auditors that they are squeaky clean. In other words, while the auditors are on-site, there will be no ghosts on the payroll, there will be no check tampering or switching, there will be no ghost vendors, and so on.

Something to Consider

Consider having the independent CPA pay a surprise visit to the client's offices on a day while the window is open, that being of course a business day during the window of opportunity for embezzlement.

The Surprise Visit

The auditors will select a day for the surprise visit at their discretion. For this surprise visit to be effective, consider the following:

1. With management's permission, of course, the auditors should have the client's bank send a cut-off bank statement directly to their offices, *not* to the client's office. This statement should include copies of the front and back of checks.

2. Have the client's credit card company send a cut-off statement to the accountant's office, as with the bank statement.

3. Transaction tests:

Purchases

Prior to the surprise visit, the accounting firm should send unknown "shoppers" to the establishment, as follows:

Cash: One of the shoppers should purchase items for cash and check to see that the items were rung up properly on the cash register and that a receipt was issued for the purchase.

Check: One of the shoppers should make a purchase with a personal check and observe that procedures were followed.

Credit: One of the shoppers should use a credit card and monitor credit card procedures.

Mail: If the client sells goods or services via the mail, test the system by carefully monitoring purchases made by credit card, check, and even cash.

Internet: If the client sells goods or services via a website, make test purchases as noted above.

4. On-site work relating to purchases:

   A. Trace the cash purchases to ensure that these transactions were not voided *after* the shopper left the premises. Obviously, if they were, a serious problem exists.

   B. Trace the credit card purchases to the cut-off credit card statement to ensure that the proper amount was recorded to the proper card.

   C. Thoroughly audit the check transactions by carefully examining the checks or check images. In particular, compare the test check endorsement stamps and bank clearinghouse stamps with other checks to ensure they that match and that someone hasn't opened up an account at another bank under the same or similar name as the client's business name.

5. Other on-site work:

   Payroll: Thoroughly investigate new employees hired after field work was concluded, to ensure that there are no ghosts on the payroll (See "Ghosts on the Payroll and Ghost Vendors" in Section 4 of this manual).

   Payroll taxes: Audit the accuracy of the payroll tax liability and actual tax deposits for federal, state, and local payroll taxes to ensure that there have been no intentional tax overpayments credited to any individual income tax withholding account.

   New vendors: Organizations should have an approved and updated vendor listing examined by the auditors during field work. New vendors added to this list should be investigated by the auditors to ensure that they actually exist and that there are no ghost vendors (See "Ghosts on the Payroll and Ghost Vendors" in Section 4 of this manual).

Tip: Examine new vendor invoices carefully. Pay close attention to and investigate new vendors that show only a post office box remittance address and no street address. Not indicating a street address on an invoice is unusual and should be investigated.

Bank reconciliations, current year: Select a random bank reconciliation prepared internally by staff and check it carefully as follows:

a. Ensure that all checks have been accounted for, and investigate any missing checks.

b. Investigate any new or unusual bank debit memoranda. A common "window of opportunity" trick is to have insurance payments, car payments, and the like paid for by debit memoranda drawn against the checking account during this period, and canceling these prior to the auditors arriving to start field work.

c. Investigate any out-of-sequence checks.

d. Test deposits.

Bank reconciliations, last month of the prior year: Here is another common scam:

Someone approves a legitimate invoice for payment early in the last month of the fiscal year and forwards the approved invoice to finance for payment. An accountant prepares the check, has it signed, and mails it to the vendor, who cashes the check accordingly. This check or check image will be in the end of the month bank statement.

Unknown to anyone, the dishonest accountant intentionally prepares a second check payable to the same vendor for the same amount of money and for the same invoice, in another check run, but places this check in the office safe. Typically, the fraudulent check will be made payable to a very clever variation of the legitimate vendor's name. For example, if the legitimate vendor is the Acme Printing *Corp.*, the second check may be made out to the Acme Printing *Co.*, and the possibility of discovering this would be very remote.

The auditors start their field work and the accountant crosses his or her fingers, hoping the auditors do not catch the double payment.

If the auditors *do* discover the double payment, typically they would bring it to the staff accountant's attention, and he would probably feign embarrassment over the double payment error, but would be able to produce the check for the second payment (it is still in the office safe), show it to the auditors, simply void the check, and correct the transaction by an adjusting journal entry.

At this point nothing looks suspicious to the auditors, because mistakes can happen, particularly at the end of the year when the accounting staff is busy with budgets, taxes, W-2 preparation, and so forth.

But what if the auditors *don't* discover the double payment, which is also possible? Simple—the perpetrator waits for field work to be concluded (the window of opportunity just opened), opens a bank account in the name of the payee of the fraudulent check, deposit the second check, waits for the funds to become available, closes the account out at that time, and pockets the money!

What is the possibility that the auditors will discover this? Very low, *because this transaction occurred on the prior year's records, which have already been audited!*

Tip: During the course of the surprise visit, revisit the end of the prior year's bank reconciliation and track the status of checks outstanding on that statement. In particular, compare the endorsement stamps appearing on these checks against other checks deposited by the same vendor, and ensure that they match.

Inventory: The surprise visit is an opportune time to examine inventory rather than waiting for field work to commence.

Tip: Open up and examine the contents of boxes of *inexpensive* inventory, particularly if there are any marks on the box. A common trick is for an employee to put an *expensive* item in a box for an inexpensive item when no one is looking and carefully place and mark the box. An accomplice could easily enter the establishment, pick up the marked box, and present it to a cashier for payment. The cashier would scan the bar code, charge the lesser amount, and watch the accomplice walk out of the store.

Tip: Assuming the client's type of inventory qualifies, of course, consider recommending that the client purchase a clear-plastic, shrink-wrap machine. If possible, wrap incoming inventory boxes in this clear plastic and safeguard the machine. Simply wrapping boxes in clear plastic greatly reduces the possibility of switching expensive and inexpensive items.

Statement of Auditing Standard No. 99 "Consideration of Fraud in a Financial Statement Audit"

Statement of Auditing Standard No. 99 "Consideration of Fraud in a Financial Statement Audit"

AN AUDIT BY an independent CPA firm is not designed to uncover fraudulent activity. The purpose of an audit is to provide reasonable assurance that the financial statements do not include any material misstatement as a result of fraudulent activity. During the auditing process, the CPA firm may uncover fraud, but this is not the reason the auditors are there.

In response to well-publicized incidents implicating auditors, the accounting profession promulgated **Statement of Auditing Standard No. 99,** "Consideration of Fraud in a Financial Statement Audit."

The primary objectives of this new auditing standard are the following:

1. Renew the public's confidence in audit quality.

2. Detect misleading financial statements.

Although the auditing CPA is still not held *responsible* or accountable for failing to detect fraud, the new standard does impose several new responsibilities on auditing CPAs in the areas of:

1. Understanding the key elements of the Fraud Triangle

2. Improved audit planning by requiring brainstorming sessions among audit team members

3. Requiring a better understanding of the client's business

4. Inquiries of key client personnel relating to existing or potential lapses in internal controls that may lead to fraud

5. Analytical procedures based on professional skepticism

6. Documentation of information gathering

The Fraud Triangle

The *cornerstone* of SAS 99 is to educate both auditors and management about the conditions that are usually present when fraud occurs, and this is best understood by taking into consideration the three corners of the Fraud Triangle, as described in Section 1:

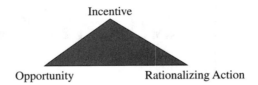

Incentive: There are endless incentives to commit a dishonest act, including financial hardship; vices such as drugs, alcohol, or gambling; employee grievances; and the desire for material goods, among others. Desperate people often take desperate action.

Opportunity: The primary opportunity to commit fraud is provided by poor or weak internal controls. An incentive to steal coupled with an opportunity in the form of poor internal controls is a dangerous combination.

Rationalizing Action: Obviously, some fraudulent acts are committed by people fully aware that they are perpetrating a crime, and their conscience produces no guilt. However, others feel they are righting a perceived wrong, such as a salary inequity, and have convinced themselves that they have earned and are owed the financial results of fraudulent acts, and therefore they are not stealing.

Once the auditing CPA understands that the elements of the Fraud Triangle are present in virtually all fraud, he or she is ready to proceed with the technical requirements of the new standard.

Improved Audit Planning

SAS 99 requires the audit team to improve the quality of the audit by mandating documented brainstorming sessions among audit personnel to assess client fraud risk.

Tip: Although it will not seem natural, the audit team members should strive to "think like a thief thinks!" during this session. With this in mind, a sample of questions that may be included in the audit team brainstorming session are:

➢ Are there any procedures that you are not comfortable with?

➢ What existing weaknesses in internal controls could be exploited?

➤ Who or what staff positions may be capable of perpetuating an embezzlement?

➤ How could revenues be misappropriated?

➤ Is collusion among staff a possibility?

➤ Is collusion among staff and customers or vendors a possibility?

➤ Which client employees should be interviewed?

➤ Has the client experienced fraud in the past, and how did the perpetrator do it?

Tip: The most effective way to conduct a brainstorming session among audit team members is to appoint a session facilitator, usually one of the senior staff. The role of the facilitator is to ensure that the golden rule of brainstorming is followed: **There are no dumb questions, observations, or suggestions, and criticism is forbidden!**

Also, remember to summarize and *document* the brainstorming session to supplement audit work papers.

Understanding the Client's Business

SAS 99 requires auditors to improve their understanding of the client's business, to better assess fraud risk. Basic building blocks to educate the auditor about the client's business include:

1. Comparison of actual versus budget revenues and expenses and investigation of material variances

2. Compilation of a five-year actual revenue and expense trend analysis and investigation of material variances

3. Utilizing outside resources—for example, comparing the client's financial statements to the financial statements of similar clients and investigating material variances

Tip: An often overlooked but excellent resource to help the auditor to better understand the client's business is the local or national association that represents your client's profession. The saying "there's an association for everything" is probably true, and very often these associations compile and sell operating ratio reports. These reports gather information, typically by budget size, for their members' balance sheets, revenues, and expenses. Compare client financials to average financials of the same budget size, and investigate material variances. These reports are excellent resources to supplement audit planning with regard to assessing risk. Finally, these reports and studies are documented audit plan proof that the CPA has taken the initiative to truly understand the nature of the client's business.

Inquiries of Client Personnel

An aspect of the Sarbanes-Oxley Act that affects SAS 99 is mandatory inquiries of certain client personnel. Some fraudulent acts would have been exposed if only people were asked if they knew of the existence of fraud. Some people won't come forth and volunteer information unless they are asked, because they are shy, reluctant to get involved, or the like.

Who should be interviewed?

The decision as to who should be asked fraud inquiry questions is made by the audit team, typically during the brainstorming session. Positions to consider include, but are not limited to:

➢ The chief executive officer
➢ The treasurer
➢ The chief financial officer
➢ The controller
➢ Accounts payable clerks
➢ Accounts receivable clerks
➢ Those handling checks or cash
➢ Security personnel
➢ Personnel who order inventory
➢ Personnel responsible for safeguarding inventory, such as warehouse personnel

And don't forget:

➢ The human resources manager (this person *always* knows what's going on!)

What questions should be asked?

The decision about what questions to ask is also a result of the brainstorming session, and is up to the judgment of the audit team.

Tip: Before making inquiries, put employees at ease and gain their confidence by telling them that auditors are *required* and have a duty to ask these questions, and that they have not been selected due to any suspicions of dishonesty.

Typical questions may include:

➢ Are you aware of the existence of fraud?
➢ Have you ever been offered expensive gifts or cash by anyone attempting to conduct business with the organization?
➢ Are you aware of any potential for fraud?
➢ Has anyone ever approached you to be an accomplice in a fraud scheme?
➢ Do you know what to do if you become aware of or are suspicious of illegal or unethical acts?
➢ Are you aware of any conflicts of interest either within or outside of the organization that could lead to collusion or increased fraud risk?

Tip: Although the Sarbanes-Oxley Act mandates whistleblower protection for public companies, it currently does not apply to nonpublic businesses or nonprofit organizations.

Depending upon the nature of the client, of course consider recommending that the client adopt a mechanism to report suspected fraud and a whistleblower policy prohibiting retaliation. Clients typically appreciate this recommendation, and documenting the suggestion in audit work papers attests that the auditors have taken seriously their responsibility to improve internal controls and assist their client in exposing fraud and reducing fraud risk. (See "Whistleblowers," in Section 3 of this handbook.)

CASE STUDY: QUITE A TRIP!

When analyzing the new client's business, the brainstorming team became aware that the client outsourced the accounting function to an accounting service. The accounting service had their client representative visit the client one day a week to pick up information, have discussions, and so forth.

The brainstorming team decided to interview this person, even though this accounting representative was not even on the client staff.

One of the questions posed to this person was, "Do any of the existing procedures make you uncomfortable?"

The accounting representative answered, "Yes, I've never been comfortable with the way they handle their company credit card transactions."

The resulting conversations and actions are very interesting:

"What makes you uncomfortable?"

"I've never seen the credit card detail. The CEO gives me a copy of the remittance advice and some codes to post to, but I've never seen the credit card detail itself."

"Where do they keep the credit card statements?"

"It's my understanding the CEO has the credit card bill sent to him personally to his home."

Based on this answer, the audit team made the decision to investigate credit card transactions very carefully. After securing the appropriate approvals, they had the credit card company forward copies of credit card statements for the prior six months directly to their offices. Their review of the statements led to uncovering a very clever and interesting embezzlement.

The audit team discovered that the CEO had been charging several thousand dollars a month to a national restaurant chain's local establishment. Through further inquiries, they later learned that the CEO's girlfriend was the assistant manager of the restaurant. Armed with this information, they contacted the internal audit department at the national restaurant's headquarters, told them something suspicious was taking place, gave them the parties' names, and asked for their cooperation in investigating the situation. A few weeks later, a representative of the national restaurant chain contacted the auditors and informed them of what they had found: It seems that when the CEO had dinner at the local restaurant, his girlfriend, the assistant manager, always waited on him personally. What he would do was give her a tip of $1,000 or more for a single dinner! Because she was in the right position as assistant manager, she simply manipulated the records for the day such that the excessive tip was directed to her personally.

All of this was discovered directly because of good interview questions and follow-up!

Analytical Procedures/Professional Skepticism

SAS 99 requires the use of analytical procedures to identify misleading financial statements that indicate fraud, basically requiring auditors to maintain a questioning mind.

As stated earlier, an excellent resource is an operating ratio report compiled by the association representing your client's profession. Compare your client's financials to national averages for the same budget bracket, and investigate significant variances.

Other analytical procedures may include:

➤ Gather a few years of *internal* monthly financial statements, and compare the same months over the different years to see if anything appears unusual.

➤ Track revenue and expense trend ratios from year to year, and investigate unusual blips.

Tip: Don't rule out that management may have *intentionally* misstated financials in order to qualify for loans, lines of credit, or the like. Embezzlement may not be present or an incentive in this case.

If Fraud Is Detected

In the event that fraud is detected within the organization, the CPA generally is not required to advise outside authorities. This is not the auditors' responsibility, unless there are some legal requirements to do so. They are, however, required to bring any issue they uncover to the appropriate level of management for resolution.

Other Areas an Auditing CPA Might Investigate

In addition to those detailed in this book, the auditing CPA will probably assess several other areas of exposure to fraud and manipulation of financial statements. These include, but are not limited to, the following schemes:

Cash Theft Schemes
➤ Cash skimming
➤ Sales skimming

➤ Unrecorded sales
➤ Sales during nonbusiness hours
➤ Theft of checks
➤ Check tampering
➤ Forged endorsements
➤ Cash register schemes
➤ Fraudulent bank reconciliations
➤ Deposit lapping
➤ Altered payees
➤ Converting stolen checks
➤ Altering receipts
➤ Fabricating sales records
➤ Altering cash counts
➤ Altering deposits
➤ False accounts
➤ Voided transactions

Billing Schemes

➤ Setting up "shell companies"
➤ Fraudulent invoicing
➤ Collusion with vendors
➤ Pass-through schemes
➤ Overbilling
➤ Kickbacks
➤ Diverting business for personal use
➤ Pay-and-return schemes
➤ False purchase orders
➤ Returning merchandise for cash

Accounts Receivable Schemes

➤ Lapping
➤ False credits
➤ False discounts
➤ Unauthorized write-offs
➤ Collection agency schemes
➤ Unauthorized credit card refunds
➤ Collusion with customers
➤ Skimming
➤ Forcing balances

➢ Debiting fictitious accounts

➢ Stolen statements

Inventory Schemes

➢ Theft and subsequent sale

➢ Over/understating on financial statements

➢ Sales returns

➢ Concealment

➢ Purchasing schemes

➢ Kickbacks

➢ Fictional vendors

➢ Padding inventory records

➢ Concealing shrinkages

➢ Falsified receiving reports

➢ Shifts between locations

➢ Diversion of inventory

➢ Short and false shipments

Fixed Asset Schemes

➢ Theft

➢ Conversion for personal use

➢ Manipulation and concealment

➢ Improper capitalization of expenses

Accounts Payable Schemes

➢ Kickbacks

➢ False or inflated vendor invoices

➢ Improper purchasing

➢ Duplicate payment schemes

➢ Theft or misappropriation of payments

➢ Contract or bidding fraud

➢ Ghost vendors

Payroll Schemes

➢ Ghosts on the payroll

➢ Commission schemes

➢ False Workers' Compensation claims

➢ Diversion of tax payments

➢ Overpayments, false wages, false pay rates

➤ Diverting wages

➤ Keeping former employees on payroll

Computer Schemes

➤ Entering false transactions

➤ Bogus file maintenance transactions

➤ Failure to enter data

➤ Altering data

➤ Manipulation of accounts

Fictitious Financial Reporting Schemes

➤ Understated liabilities

➤ Recording fictitious assets

➤ Improper capitalization of expenses

➤ Sham transactions

➤ Improper revenue recognition

➤ Overstated accounts receivables

➤ Overly complex transactions

Debt/Equity Schemes

➤ Unauthorized borrowing

➤ Division of loan proceeds

➤ Stock and dividend manipulation

Expense Account Schemes

➤ Overstated reimbursement requests

➤ Altered supporting documentation

➤ Fictitious receipts

➤ Multiple reimbursements

➤ Claiming expenses paid by others

➤ Substituting expensive air fare itineraries for those of discount carriers

Other Important Areas of Concern

➤ Asset flipping

➤ Credit card exposures

➤ Conflicts of interest

➤ Employee lifestyles

3

Essential Internal Control and Administrative Procedures to Avoid Embezzlement

The Background Check

IN OUR LITIGIOUS society, it is becoming increasingly difficult to get honest references from previous employers for new employee candidates. In fact, when a company contacts a prospective employee's prior employer, the organization will typically only provide verification of the person's title and the duration of the employee's term of employment.

This makes hiring very difficult today. It means that, in the hiring process, employers have to rely almost exclusively on the accuracy of the individual's application or résumé, plus the honesty of the individual during the interview stage. Ultimately, you can assume that this means you will know virtually nothing about your new hires.

The only sure way to find out what you need to know about the prospect is to request permission to perform a background check. While you wouldn't expect, or impose, a background check for every position within your organization, you should consider it for key positions, particularly those in finance and those that involve handling checks, credit cards, and cash.

You must ask the potential employee for permission to conduct a background check, and that permission should be in writing. Of course, prospective employees have the right to deny permission and, legally, this is not supposed to be taken into consideration during the hiring process. If you have any doubt at all, check with your attorney.

It is critically important to receive permission from prospective employees (always check with your attorney first for guidance) to conduct a thorough background check for the following positions:

> *All* employees in accounting and finance
> Other employees handling cash, checks, or credit cards
> The human resources manager
> Other positions that management feels are key

There are services such as private investigative firms whose business it is to conduct these background checks; this fee is very affordable and offsets the possible risk of hiring the wrong person.

At a minimum, a background check should include the following:

1. **Criminal Background Check**

   If an individual has been convicted of a crime, the matter is public record. Obviously, a check of criminal activity is vital with regard to the positions named.

   Criminal background checks should be conducted at the following:

   > The state of residence
   > The state of employment
   > The states adjacent to the states of residence or employment
   > Other states noted on the prospect's application, such as prior employment states, and the like

2. **Credit Check**

   Credit checks are very easy to obtain, and the three primary credit agencies are:

   > Experian
   > Equifax
   > TransUnion

   Note: See "Identity Theft," Section 6 of this manual, for contact information on these credit agencies.

   Any problem with credit history is a cause for alarm, but obviously people with *serious* credit problems could become desperate and should *never* be hired for key positions.

3. **References**

   A check on references is important, but realistically, no one would include a bad reference on an application. Compounding this is the fact that most employers are only going to release information such as the person's title and length of employment, due to fear of litigation.

Tip: As stated, no one is going to list a poor reference on a résumé, but any significant time periods *between* jobs may indicate a problem at an unnamed employer.

4. **Social Security Number**

A verification of an applicant's Social Security number is important, because it is common for someone to be hired under a fictitious number or someone else's Social Security number.

Why?

A common ruse is to be hired using someone else's Social Security number and file a W-4 with several dependents, resulting in little or no federal and state income taxes being withheld. At the same time, this person could be collecting unemployment, food stamps, and other subsidies from the state. Important: It is now possible to verify Social Security numbers directly via the Social Security Administration. However, this verification is offered only *after* someone is hired.

5. **Driving Record**

Surprisingly, it is important to check driving records through the Department of Motor Vehicles.

Why?

A poor driving record would not preclude hiring someone, but *don't* have the person run errands and the like for the organization. If this person unfortunately gets into an accident during the course of the work day, while doing business for the organization, you can count on the business itself to be named in any resulting legal action.

6. **Education and Degrees Attained**

Community colleges, colleges, and universities will verify academic credentials as well as grade transcripts. The education verification will expose any embellished educational background.

7. **Professional Credentials**

If the employee candidate has professional credentials such as attorney, CPA, industry certifications, and so forth, these credentials are easily checked. Ensure that the individual actually has these credentials and that licenses are current.

Additionally, it may be wise to include the following:

8. **Drug Testing**

9. **FBI Fingerprint Check**

Remember that you have to get the prospective employee's permission to conduct a background check. Also, be certain to have a knowledgeable labor law attorney review a draft of the permission form before implementing the form, to ensure it meets federal and state laws.

A *draft* of a Permission to Conduct a Background Check may appear as follows:

Permission to Conduct
Background Checks

I ___(employee name)___ do hereby give permission to conduct a background check both before and anytime subsequent to employment.

I understand this background check may include the following areas:

➤ Criminal
➤ Credit
➤ References
➤ Social Security Number
➤ Driving Record
➤ Education and Degrees Attained
➤ Professional Credentials
➤ Drug Testing
➤ FBI Fingerprint Check

I also acknowledge and understand that if any information included on my Application for Employment, Résumé, Curriculum Vitae or any other document related to my employment is later found to be false, my employment may be terminated immediately for cause.

Employee Signature _____

Date _____

Witness Name _____

Witness Signature _____

Date _____

Conditions of Employment Agreement

The necessity for thorough background checks was covered earlier in this section. The Conditions of Employment agreement is another important employment document that employees should sign before hire.

The most important elements to be included in this document are:

1. **Termination for Erroneous Statements**

   A potential employee's application and résumé will typically include education information, prior employment positions, professional credentials, references, and other important information. Additionally, the application form should inquire if the applicant has ever been convicted of a felony. Once the employee signs the application, that person attests that the information is truthful.

   Part of the Conditions of Employment document should clearly state that the organization has reserved the right of termination of employment if any of this information is later proven false.

2. **Offers and Acceptance of Gifts**

   It is common for an unscrupulous vendor to unethically or sometimes even illegally try to influence employees by offering them gifts. Obviously, trivial gift offers such as candy during the holidays is no cause for concern, but offers of expensive gifts and cash constitute bribes, and it is important to include in the Conditions of Employment agreement that such gift offers must be reported to management.

3. **Management Day**

   The Conditions of Employment agreement should state that management has reserved the right to direct an employee not to report to work on a day at *management's* discretion (with pay). The employee acknowledges that management has reserved the right to have another employee assume his or her responsibilities on this day, sit at his or her desk and review mail, and the like.

   Additionally, a management representative (with a witness) has reserved the right to inspect the contents of the employee's desk, review websites the employee visits, review emails, and so on.

4. **Uninterrupted Vacation**

   The Conditions of Employment agreement should state that management has reserved the right to *require* employees to take at least one full week of vacation per year.

   Additionally, as noted in item 3 above, during this week management may have another employee sit at the absent employee's desk, inspect desk contents, turn on the computer, and so forth.

5. **Sick Days**

   The Conditions of Employment agreement should also note that the same actions that management may take on the Management Day and during Uninterrupted Vacation also apply to sick days.

6. **Involuntary Terminations/Leaves of Absence**

   The Conditions of Employment agreement should state clearly the following:

   ➤ Discussions regarding involuntary terminations and leaves of absence will *not* take place in the employee's office, cubicle, or similar location. Rather, the discussion will be held in an office of the management team or a neutral location such as a conference room, library, or the like. Remember that the offender's office probably contains important evidence that the offender should not have access to.

   ➤ At a minimum, termination discussions should *always* include a witness selected by management to verify exactly what was said during the discussion, and the manager and witness should prepare notes immediately after the discussion and record important statements, actions, and so on. Additionally, reserve the right to have other parties attend, if deemed necessary, such as a lawyer, CPA, police officer, or the like.

   If a man has to confront a woman, the witness should be another woman. If a woman finds it necessary to confront a man, the witness should be another man. This, of course, lessens the chance of being accused of any sexual impropriety.

7. **Surrender of Organization Intellectual Property**

   Work produced by an employee during the course of employment, such as correspondence, reports, studies, books, or articles, is considered intellectual property and *is the property of the organization*. This fact should be communicated to the prospective employee to avoid any misunderstandings at termination.

8. **Surrender of Customer Information**

   Many employees have access to sensitive customer information such as credit card numbers, checking account numbers, Social Security numbers, addresses, telephone numbers, and the like. The Conditions of Employment agreement should state that this information may not be removed from the office under any circumstances, but particularly at termination of employment.

9. **Immediate Removal from Office**

   The Conditions of Employment agreement should be clear in stating that, immediately upon termination:

   ➤ The employee will surrender such items as door keys, credit cards, and the like.

> The employee will not be allowed to return to his or her office, cubicle, or other work area. If the employee needs essential personal items such as a purse, wallet, car keys, *two* other employees will retrieve them for the employee (requiring two other employees to retrieve these items eliminates accusations such as theft).

> The employee will then be escorted directly out of the building.

> Other personal effects (photos, pictures, etc.) will be gathered by *two* other employees, and these items will be later delivered to the employee's residence via courier.

10. **Prosecution**

The document should state very clearly that in the event an embezzlement or fraud is proven, the organization *will prosecute* the offending employee, regardless of the dollar amount involved, to the full extent of the law.

This threat of prosecution is an effective deterrent against fraud. If the employee has any questions concerning prosecution, explain that a prosecution may result in a criminal record, and this would obviously affect future employment at other organizations.

A Conditions of Employment agreement document may appear as follows:

Conditions of Employment Agreement Form

I, __(employee name)__, an employee of __(organization)__ acknowledge and agree to the following Conditions of Employment:

1. Termination for Erroneous Statements

I understand that if any information provided by me and noted on my original APPLICATION FOR EMPLOYMENT or related documents provided by me such as a RÉSUMÉ or CURRICULUM VITAE is later proven to be false, these misstatements are grounds for termination of employment.

These misstatements include, but are not limited to, education, professional credentials, prior employers, prior positions, job responsibilities, references, arrest record, etc.

2. Offers of Gifts by Vendors

I understand that acceptance of offers of expensive gifts or cash by vendors will be considered acceptance of a bribe and may be cause for disciplinary action or termination of employment.

I also understand that I have a responsibility to report such offers to the appropriate level of management.

3. Management Day

I understand that management has reserved the right to direct me not to report to work on a day of management's discretion (with pay).

I also understand that management has reserved the right to direct another employee to assume my responsibilities, sit at my desk, review mail, etc.

I further understand that a management representative and a witness may inspect the contents of my desk, review my computer files including websites I have been visiting, email messages, etc.

I agree to abide by the provisions of the EMPLOYEE HANDBOOK and if unallowable items such as alcohol, illegal drugs, pornography, etc. are discovered, this will be grounds for immediate termination of employment for cause.

4. Uninterrupted Vacation

I understand that I am required to take at least one full week of uninterrupted vacation per year and that management may mandate this vacation if I fail to schedule it voluntarily.

On this time off, I also understand that management has reserved the right to have another employee assume my responsibilities, inspect the contents of my desk as well as other action noted in Item 3 above.

5. Sick Days

I understand that the actions management has reserved the right to take in Items 3 and 4 noted in this document also apply to any sick days I may take.

6. Involuntary Terminations/Leaves of Absence

I understand that discussions concerning my involuntary termination or leave of absence will take place at a location other than my office, cubicle, etc. such as an office of management, conference room, library, etc.

I also understand that this discussion will include a witness and management has reserved the right to also include attorneys, CPAs, police officers, etc. at their discretion.

7. Surrender of Organization Intellectual Property

I understand that all work products that I produce during my employment, as well as works-in-progress, are the organization's intellectual property. Upon my termination, whether voluntary or involuntary, this property and supporting documents will not be removed from the office under any circumstances, and I may not use this information for any purpose without the express written permission of management.

This property includes, but is not limited to:

➤ Correspondence
➤ Reports
➤ Studies
➤ Books
➤ Articles
➤ Accounting Records
➤ Videos

8. Surrender of Customer/Employee Information

I understand that I may come into contact with sensitive information regarding customers and employees, and in this respect I agree to keep this information confidential and I understand this information may not leave the office for any reason.

This information includes, but is not limited to:

➤ Credit card information
➤ Bank account information
➤ Social Security numbers
➤ Telephone numbers
➤ Addresses
➤ Mailing lists
➤ Prospect lists

9. Immediate Removal from Office

I understand and agree to the following in the event of my involuntary termination or leave of absence:

➤ I will surrender such items as organization door keys, credit cards, etc. at management's request.
➤ I will be escorted directly out of the office and will not be allowed to return to my personal office, cubicle, etc.
➤ In the event I require essential personal items such as a purse, wallet, car keys, etc., two employees will recover these items from my office for me.
➤ Nonessential personal effects such as photographs, etc. will be gathered by two employees and these items will be delivered to my residence via courier.

10. Prosecution

I understand that if fraud or embezzlement are proven, management may proceed with prosecution to the full extent of the law, regardless of the dollar amount of the incident.

I also understand that prosecution may result in a criminal record that may affect my prospects for future employment elsewhere.

11. Background Check

I understand that, in accordance with the *Permissions to Conduct Background Checks Form*, the organization has reserved the right to conduct background checks anytime subsequent to my unemployment.

I hereby state that I have read and understand this Conditions of Employment agreement and the Employee Handbook and agree to abide by the conditions therein.

Employee Name _____

Employee Signature _____

Date _____

Management Representative Name _____

Management Representative Signature _____

Date _____

Note: This material is not intended as legal advice. Before implementing these suggestions, be certain to have them reviewed by a competent employment law attorney familiar with your state and federal employment laws.

Tip: When the employee signs and dates the agreement, have Human Resources make a copy of it and place the *copy* in the employee's personnel file. Place the original in a location to which the employee has no access, such as a safe deposit box or safe.

As stated elsewhere in this handbook, it is very important to protect the original document, because it may be evidence in the event of a criminal proceeding. In the event of an incident, if the offending employee removed this document, it could weaken a criminal case because a defense attorney could assert that the employee was never made aware of the ramifications of his or her actions and would not have proceeded with the fraud if he or she had known it would result in dire consequences.

Case Study: The Value of Implementing the Management Day Policy:

A CEO owned a small chain of automobile repair shops, and each shop was run by a general manager. The general managers were eligible for a sizable year-end bonus based on the net profit of the store for the year.

Unknown to the CEO, one of the general managers concocted a scheme to inflate the store's net profit and hence increase his bonus. What he would do was convince an unknowing customer that an expensive part was needed to repair his car. The customer, assuming that the general manager was honest, agreed to the repair and paid the bill when it was presented. The invoice included a bill for the expensive part and labor, but the part was never installed. This scheme significantly increased the store's net profit, of course, because it billed for parts with no cost, and labor that was not actually provided.

The CEO decided to implement the Management Day policy and directed the offending general manager to take a day off with pay. The general manager was prohibited from coming to the shop this day and his responsibilities were assumed by the assistant manager.

On this day off, one of the unknowingly bilked customers came to the shop complaining he still had problems with his car. He presented his receipt to the assistant manager, who discovered that the expensive part was never installed, exposing the scam.

Conflicts of Interest

It is inevitable that conflicts of interest will arise in an organization. This can occur on all levels, whether the board of directors or staff.

Therefore, everyone who works for, or represents, the organization (including board members, staff, committee members, and so forth) must sign a Conflict of Interest form.

This serves to raise the level of awareness that the organization does not tolerate or defend conflicts of interest. Additionally, this will encourage reporting of all real or perceived conflicts of interest. For the protection of everyone involved, these conflicts should be brought to the attention of the level of authority necessary for consideration, resolution, and direction.

Conflict of Interest Form

I have been informed of this organization's policy regarding conflicts of interest. I agree to bring to the attention of the proper level of authority any real, or perceived, conflicts of interest that may arise during the course of my tenure with this organization.

Such conflicts include, but are not limited to, personal or professional affiliations, relationships with family and friends, dealings with other organizations or businesses, political considerations, or relationships with other boards of directors.

Additionally, I agree to abide by the direction and decision of management. I understand that failure to advise management of such conflicts may result in disciplinary action, termination of employment, or removal from my position.

Name _____

Position_____

Signature _____

Date _____

Nepotism

Employing relatives is usually a very bad idea. Initially, it may seem to be a quick solution to a hiring issue, but it may very well backfire. Over and above the normal day-to-day tensions that can happen in the workplace, collusion is much more likely to occur among family members than among unrelated employees.

To protect your company, you probably should have a nepotism policy across the board. If that is not feasible, or desirable, you should consider, at the very least, a modified, department-specific policy. This will effectively prevent and prohibit the employment of family members in any area where you feel most vulnerable and, in particular, the accounting function.

The policy should also state that family members will not be hired for, or transferred into, positions where they will have direct or indirect supervision of one another.

This will save you a lot of headaches and human resources problems in the future.

As with all forms and policies suggested in this manual, review the Nepotism Policy and Nepotism form with a competent attorney.

Sample Nepotism Policy

It is the policy of the company that no employee shall be employed in a position in which the employee must report directly or indirectly to a family member (immediate or extended family), spouse, partner, significant other, or someone with whom the employee lives.

If two employees should become spouses, partners, significant others, or choose to live together, one must resign if one reports directly or indirectly to the other. Failure to voluntarily resign will result in the involuntary termination of one of the parties at the discretion of management.

Employee Name _____

Employee Signature _____

Date _____

Whistleblowers

There is evidence that the only reason some fraudulent acts were exposed was whistleblowers—someone came forward and reported known or suspected illegal activity.

With this in mind, an aspect of the Sarbanes-Oxley Act of 2002, prohibiting retaliation against whistleblowers, should be addressed.

As of the copyright date of this handbook, the Sarbanes-Oxley Act requires only public companies to comply with this policy. However, other businesses, non-profit organizations, and the like should give serious consideration to implementing a mechanism for reporting known or suspected fraud and a whistleblower protection policy prohibiting retaliation. A mechanism for reporting suspicious activity should be well thought out and written.

The policy itself should be included in the Employee Handbook, and employees should also be required to sign a form further strengthening the spirit of the policy.

Employee Handbook Policy

"All employees have a duty to report on suspected fraud or unethical activity to the appropriate level of management. Such reporting will be strictly anonymous and confidential.

Additionally, any retaliation against any employee who has reported on a suspicious activity will not be tolerated and the offending employee will be subject to disciplinary action and possible termination."

Review the Whistleblower Policy and form with a competent attorney.

Employee Responsibility to Report Fraudulent or Unethical Activity Form

An unfortunate aspect of our society is that fraudulent and unethical activity is a reality all organizations are subject to, and our organization is no exception.

The organization has a policy whereby all employees are required to report known or suspected fraud or unethical activity in a confidential manner, and retaliation against such employees is strictly forbidden and grounds for possible termination of employment.

Anonymous Reporting

All employees who become aware of actual or suspected fraud or unethical conduct have an obligation to report such activity to the appropriate level of management. This information will be held strictly confidential and the reporting employee will remain anonymous.

Retaliation Prohibited

If management becomes aware of any retaliation in any form against an employee reporting actual or suspected fraudulent or unethical activity, the offending employee will be subject to disciplinary action including possible termination of employment.

By signing this document, I acknowledge that I am aware that I have an obligation to report real or suspected fraudulent or unethical activity to the appropriate level of management, and that such reporting will be held strictly confidential and anonymous. I also acknowledge that retaliation in any form taken against such an employee will not be tolerated, and such action will be grounds for disciplinary action including possible termination.

Employee Name _____

Employee Signature _____

Date _____

Witness Name_____

Witness Signature_____

Date _____

Noncompete Agreements

Every company has competition. But you don't want to have a competitor on your staff. Therefore, it's important to have every individual associated with your company sign a Noncompete agreement.

Noncompete agreements should specify that employees should not be employed by, or have any type of relationship with, *a competing organization.* This prohibition will cover the period of time that the employee remains with you. Upon termination, the former employee must surrender all materials, documents, or information that would be of value to the competing organization. This information typically includes, but is not limited to:

➤ Financial information
➤ Sales materials
➤ Customer information
➤ Member information
➤ Mailing lists
➤ Equipment
➤ Confidential information
➤ Legal documents
➤ Personnel records
➤ Business plans
➤ Marketing plans
➤ Competitive data
➤ Original documents of any kind

Noncompete Agreement Form

I acknowledge that, during the course of my employment, I am prohibited from concurrent employment, or any other relationship with, any real or perceived competitor of the company.

I also agree that, upon termination of my employment, I will surrender to the company all information, documents, or materials that would be of benefit to any competing organization.

I also agree that I will not discuss any confidential information, knowledge, or data that I obtained during the course of my employment.

Name _____

Title/Department _____

Signature _____

Date _____

Supervisor_____

Signature _____

Date _____

Review this form with a competent attorney before implementation.

Confidentiality of Information

In almost any position in a company, an employee will be entrusted with confidential information. Consequently, it's in the best interests of all involved to have everyone sign a Confidentiality agreement.

Confidential information includes, but is not limited to:

➤ Financial statements

➤ Salaries and wages

➤ Contracts with vendors

➤ Lease information

➤ Credit information

➤ Banking relationships

➤ Insurance information

➤ Customer or member data

➤ Legal matters

➤ Personnel concerns

➤ Bid information

➤ Tax information and returns

➤ Personnel records

➤ Budget information

➤ Business plans

➤ New product development

➤ Competitive assessments

➤ Marketing plans and strategies

➤ Affiliations

The basic agreement should be simple and brief. Make sure that you review the agreement with your attorney to ensure that what you are implementing covers all aspects of confidentiality important to your company. At the same time, it is important that you do not inadvertently intrude on anyone's personal rights, so review the Confidentiality of Information form with a competent attorney.

Confidentiality Agreement Form

It is the policy of this company to ensure that its operations, activities, and affairs are kept strictly confidential.

In the event that, during your employment, you acquire confidential or proprietary information and/or you are involved in confidential matters, it is understood that you will hold such information in strict confidence. Such information is to be discussed on a need-to-know basis only and exclusively with the staff person in authority.

Confidential information includes, but is not limited to:

- Financial statements
- Salaries and wages
- Contracts with vendors
- Lease information
- Credit information
- Banking relationships
- Insurance information
- Customer or member data
- Legal matters
- Personnel concerns

- Bid information
- Tax information and returns
- Personnel records
- Budget information
- Business plans
- New product development
- Competitive assessments
- Marketing plans and strategies
- Affiliations

By signing this agreement, I agree to the Confidentiality Policy and acknowledge violations of confidentiality will be subject to disciplinary action and possible termination.

Name _____

Title_____

Signature _____ Date _____

Supervisor_____

Signature _____ Date _____

Bonding Issues

It is extremely important for all organizations to have a Fidelity Bond, also known as Employee Dishonesty Insurance. The purpose of bonding your employees is to protect the organization, as a whole, in the event of internal embezzlement.

When you look into getting bonded, you need to make certain that the bond is adequate. You also need to know who is, and who is not, covered on the bond, and you should have a predetermined plan of action to follow in the event of a claim.

Who Should Be Covered?

It goes without saying the CEO, CFO, and other key employees with a lot of responsibility and control, should be included. In addition, I firmly believe that every employee who has *anything* to do with money coming into, or money going out of, the organization should be included on the Fidelity Bond. That even includes mailroom employees, front desk personnel, accounts receivable/payable clerks, and all check signers.

Officers and directors are often excluded from coverage. Know your bond and who is covered. Don't assume coverage for an important position. The coverage might not exist, particularly on your Chief Financial Officer, and you may be out on a limb without a net. (Refer to "Wire Transfers," in Section 4, for an example of what can happen if you are not careful with the details of your Fidelity Bond.)

How Much Is Enough?

The amount of the coverage, and the deductible per claim, will differ with each company. The two major factors to consider are the nature of the business and the level of its potential exposure. You should do a study to determine what a potential loss might total and ascertain the amount of the deductible you are prepared to pay per claim. Obviously, the amount of coverage and the deductible will dictate the cost of your coverage. Don't let cost, however, interfere with your good judgment. Protect your company and yourself.

When You Make a Claim

You must read the Fidelity Bond Policy. Too many of my clients rely on a staff person to check the policy details, while they look at the big picture. While this may be appropriate sometimes, it isn't when it comes to liability coverage. You need to thoroughly discuss all the provisions with your insurance agent. Legitimate claims are sometimes disallowed if the organization, among other things, fails to advise the insurance company in the proper manner, or fails to secure a timely police report.

Once the organization has flow-charted the cash trail and decided on the amount of coverage, you should meet with the insurance agent to discuss all the details, including excluded positions and claims procedures. Then you should determine how you are going to handle claims and the steps to be taken in the event of a claim. This will go a long way toward avoiding surprises in the event of a problem.

Other Issues

Finally, ensure that there are no relationships with other organizations that *require* the bond be at a certain monetary value. It is common for granting agencies to require the bond be set at the amount of the grant, banks often require set bond amounts, and so forth.

Tip: Explain to employees what a Fidelity Bond is and emphasize that when the organization subrogates its rights to the insurance company, the insurance carrier *will* prosecute.

Signers on Bank Accounts

In case you haven't noticed, most of the perpetrators of fraud work in the accounting department. Most of the examples throughout the book demonstrate this.

Therefore, it should come as no surprise that I recommend strongly that accounting personnel should never be check signers or wire transfer agents. Individuals who have access to checks, process checks, verify bank reconciliations, compute payroll, or handle any other financial function should never be authorized signers. It is much too tempting.

The best procedure for processing checks:

Step 1.   The invoice is approved for payment.

Step 2.   A check request form is completed.

Step 3.   The CEO approves the check request.

Step 4.   The check request is forwarded to accounting.

Step 5.   Accounting processes the check.

Step 6.   The CEO signs the check.

Step 7.   A second designated employee (who does not approve the payment and is not in the accounting department) should cosign the check.

With this system, the company has four people involved in processing a check: the approver, the accountant, the CEO, and the second check signer. That makes a fraudulent transaction significantly more difficult to perpetrate.

Two-Signature Checks

Two signatures should be required on every check. This is vital for administrative and internal control purposes.

Requiring the second signature on every check simply means an extra pair of eyes is looking at each transaction. That limits the probability of either an honest error (such as an incorrect amount or unintentional double payment) or an embezzlement. It seriously limits frauds and embezzlement because collusion would have to be present, and that is rare. It is extremely risky for one individual to approach another individual to enter into a theft scheme.

Consequently, if there is embezzlement even when two signatures are required, it's very likely that the second signature is a forgery. Believe it or not, this is good for the organization. Forgery is a felony and is easily proved. Therefore, you have an easier legal case than if you are trying to prove theft.

Is One Signature Ever Good Enough?

How about requiring just one signature for checks written for small amounts, such as under $500? Not a good idea. It sounds as though it would help lighten the administrative load, but it can backfire. And I can attest to that.

During a consulting arrangement with a client to evaluate their internal controls, I suggested that they require two signatures on every check. Ignoring my advice, they decided to set up a policy that only required two signatures for checks over $1,000. Any amount under that would only require one signature.

Sounds reasonable. Right? Wrong.

A few weeks later, I sent them an invoice for $2,700 for my consulting fee. My payment came in the form of three checks, in the amount of $900 each and signed by only one person. The staff had found a way to expedite their check-processing procedure.

This is a great example of how the spirit of the policy varies from reality. The flow chart for processing a check should be as follows:

Check-Processing Procedure

➤ Invoice is approved for payment.

➤ Check request form is prepared.

➤ The CEO approves/signs the numbered check request form.

➤ Check request form is forwarded to accounting.

➤ Accounting processes the check.

➤ The check is signed by two authorized individuals.

➤ The check is mailed.

➤ The bank statements are sent to the CEO's home (or P.O. box) for review.

➤ The CEO forwards the reviewed bank statements to accounting for reconciliation.

In this scenario, two people are required for every check issued, which greatly reduces the probability of fraud.

Unless the organization is extremely large (and then you should have a computerized system), never utilize a check-signing machine or a signature stamp. Besides the obvious lack of internal control that results from these devices, fraudulent checks often involve forging a check signer's signature. This is a felony act that is easier to prove than the unauthorized use of a check-signing machine or signature stamp.

Lockbox

Most banks have a Lockbox Service, and businesses that receive checks and credit card transactions through the mail should give serious consideration to utilizing this service, so that organization employees don't come into contact with original checks.

Lockbox is an arrangement whereby remittances to an organization are actually sent directly to the organization's bank, rather than to the organization's physical address. Typically, the organization mails invoices to customers and provides an addressed remittance envelope. This envelope usually has the organization's name but, unknown to the remitter, the address is actually the bank's address.

The bank receives the remittances, makes a copy of the check, and deposits the original check. The copy of the check, envelope, and data in the envelope are forwarded to the organization with a validated bank deposit slip.

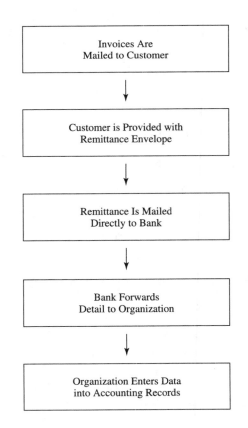

Once again, with regard to internal controls, Lockbox is very effective, because employees do not come into contact with original checks, virtually eliminating theft of these remittances.

There is an additional benefit to using Lockbox: Generally, most businesses receive remittances on a business day, but these receipts are not physically deposited until the next business day. If Lockbox is used, the bank deposits the receipts on the day they were received, and if the Lockbox account at the bank is an interest-bearing account, the organization will benefit from an additional day's interest. If an entire year's receipts benefit from this additional interest, this revenue will significantly offset the bank's fee for the Lockbox Service. When this interest earned factors in weekends and holidays, the financial benefit of using Lockbox really makes sense.

Positive Pay

Positive Pay is a relatively new service offered by most commercial banks, and it is probably the best internal control over check disbursements an organization can employ.

There are variations of this service, but basically:

1. The bank provides the organization with Positive Pay software.

2. The organization loads the software on its computer.

3. As checks are processed, important information is exported to the bank via a modem, compact disk, or other means.

4. As checks are presented to the bank, the information forwarded to the bank by the organization is matched against the checks. If the information presented does not match exactly, the bank will not honor the check without the organization's approval.

The essential information Positive Pay checks for includes:

➤ Payee is correct.

➤ The amount of the check is correct.

➤ Checks have not been duplicated and cashed more than once.

➤ Voided (Stop Payment) checks have not been presented for payment.

➤ There are no out-of-sequence checks.

➤ Expired checks have not been presented for payment.

Positive Pay, coupled with other effective internal control policies, such as requiring two check signers, prohibiting checks from being made payable to acronyms, prohibiting employees in the finance department from being signers, requiring check requests, having an independent review of bank statements, and so forth, will go a long way toward preventing check fraud.

Deposit Security and Restrictive Endorsements

As they arrive, checks should be put immediately under lock and key. They should never be left out in the open, on countertops or desks, where other employees or customers might have access to them. It has become very simple for a knowledgeable person to divert such checks for their own use.

Check This Out

Consider this scenario. The mail carrier leaves the day's mail on the countertop in the reception area. A new customer walks in and sees the pile of mail. Seizing the opportunity, the customer simply picks up the mail and walks out.

In the pile, there are several checks made payable to the ABC Service Company. Any embezzler knows that he or she can open a new bank account anywhere in the United States, in the name of the ABC Service Company. The embezzler can use the stolen checks as the initial deposit. Monitoring the availability of funds online, this person could write a check drawn on the newly opened account and end up with a lot of cash.

Checks Require Immediate Action

It never ceases to amaze me how often companies sit on checks before processing them. These checks are payments; delaying deposits can mean a loss of interest income, a chance that you are holding a bad check, or an opportunity for someone to execute a check fraud. So my first piece of advice is: **When a check arrives, act fast.**

Make sure *everyone* on staff (not just accounting personnel) knows that checks are the lifeblood of the business and, therefore, they take priority over everything else. Without those payments in your bank account, you just might not have anything else. So checks come first. (And, in my opinion, billing is a close second.)

Make certain that the mail is handled properly. Instruct the mail carrier (usually it's the same person, coming at the same time every day) that mail should not be left on a desktop. Have a buzzer to alert the backup person to the receptionist that the mail has arrived, or have a special, secure container where the mail can be placed.

Your Check Endorsement

Once the checks have been sorted from the regular mail, they should be immediately endorsed with a For Deposit Only stamp, a restrictive endorsement preventing them from being cashed. This prevents checks from being diverted, cashed, or used as a deposit. Altering an endorsed check is very difficult. (By the way, you should do this on all your personal and payroll checks as well. Just hand-write the information on the back, including For Deposit Only, and your check is safe until you get to the bank.)

Your endorsement stamp should spell out your organization's full legal name, under the words For Deposit Only. Never use an acronym. To keep your banking information confidential, you should *not* include the name of your company's bank or your account number on the endorsement stamp. That way, no one can find out this information from a cleared check. For example, assume your organization has been targeted by a clever scam artist. This individual purchases something from your organization with a personal check that was approved with a Telecheck machine. This person probably doesn't want or need what he or she has purchased, what they really want is their canceled check back when they get their next personal bank statement in the mail. If your endorsement stamp has your bank account number on it, *they* now have your bank account number, because it is on the back of their personal check. Armed with your account number, it is simple for the thief to print checks for a fraudulent entity with your account number! It can take a long time before this scam is discovered, and once it is discovered, the defrauded business has to close out the account and deal with the bank to recover the funds.

Sample endorsement stamp

FOR DEPOSIT ONLY
YOUR COMPANY NAME
(e.g., American Crayon Association, Inc.)

Once the checks have been endorsed and the deposit prepared, put everything under lock and key.

Check Deposit Security Procedure

➢ Checks are endorsed immediately with proper endorsement stamp.

➢ Deposit slip is prepared.

➢ Deposits are taken to the bank (or put in the safe until they can be deposited).

Often companies have multiple accounts. Consequently, the checks that are received are made payable to different payees. This makes endorsements more challenging. I advise initially depositing these properly stamped checks in your main bank and then transferring the funds to the other banks later. At a minimum, at least initially stamp these checks with a For Deposit Only stamp without the individual account name.

In all cases, endorsed checks should be forwarded directly to the finance department, not to the department responsible for the sale. If other departments need these checks, issue copies of the checks. Never release your originals to anyone but accounting.

A Note on Lockbox

I must remind you how valuable the Lockbox Service can be. If an organization uses a bank's Lockbox Service, employees never come into contact with original checks, thereby eliminating the possibility of diverting, altering, or cashing checks. See "Lockbox," in this section of this manual.

Check Stock

If you use the type of check stock that can't be scanned or that smears easily (if someone attempts to erase the figures), then you are ahead of the game. In fact, you are so far ahead, you can move on to the next chapter. If you don't use this type of stock, you need to know about scams that can occur. So read on.

Read This and Weep

In the following check-scanning scam, a check was made payable to the ABC Publishing Company in the amount of $20,000.

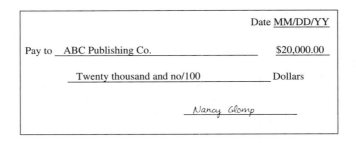

Someone, somewhere along the line, intercepted the check before it got to the publishing company. He effectively scanned the original check onto the same type of check paper stock. The scan was so perfect that it was hard to tell the difference between the original check and the eleven scanned copies.

The person who retrieved and scanned the check was part of a group of conspirators who were set up in several different states. These conspirators, each in possession of a scanned check, easily opened up bank accounts in their respective states, under the name of ABC Publishing. They used the scanned $20,000 checks as their "initial" deposit to activate the accounts.

They monitored their accounts electronically and waited for the deposit to clear the bank, making the funds available. Once this occurred, they quickly used the temporary checks supplied by the bank to access the funds. $220,000 was stolen in less than ten days, before anyone was aware of what had happened.

A Check Is Only As Good As the Stock It's Printed On

It is very important to invest in the type of check stock that can't be scanned. This kind of stock is encoded with the words "VOID" or "NOT AN ORIGINAL DOCUMENT," which are not noticeable to the naked eye. They will, however, appear on the face of the copy of the scanned check.

It's also surprisingly easy to erase words and numbers on checks and then replace them with different amounts. To prevent this from happening, you should invest in the type of check stock that smears very easily if someone attempts to erase the amounts.

All of this may seem very simple, and it is. It doesn't take much to protect yourself from a very basic, but devastating, scam.

Tip: If possible, consider a policy whereby the payee's *address* is printed on every check under the payee's name. Why? If someone steals or intercepts checks and attempts to open an account under the same name in another state, this should be noticed and viewed as suspicious by an alert bank representative.

Cash Transactions

If your business has cash transactions of any kind, you must have a method to ensure that all the cash you receive goes into the till and stays there. By their very nature, cash transactions are hard to control. Their lack of audit trail makes securing transactions even more challenging. As a precaution, most companies have a policy that specifies that all purchases be accompanied by a receipt. But that doesn't afford much protection in the long run.

Imagine that someone comes into a local chamber of commerce to purchase a directory. In all likelihood, the front desk is occupied by a clerk with little, or no, direct supervision. The customer pays cash for the book and is given a receipt.

Is there any guarantee that the cash will stay in the till? Not really. The employee could easily void the transaction by processing a refund, and then pocket the money.

The best way to prevent this, and other similar situations, is to discuss your concerns with your CPA firm. They will have some ideas that you can institute that will pay off. One will be to have a firm, written policy that all cash transactions require receipts.

And, best of all, they might suggest sending out a "secret shopper" who visits the chamber, pays cash for a directory, and is given a receipt. Then you can check the day's receipts to ensure that the transaction wasn't voided. If it was voided, you know that the individual who voided the sale (the clerk or someone else in the office) is pocketing the money. If the transaction was not voided, you can be comfortable with the knowledge that your policy is being followed and that the employee who handled the transaction is honest.

After the good news, also follow up with a short employee meeting the following day. First, discuss routine matters. Then call the clerk who processed the transaction to the front of the room. Announce that the customer who purchased the directory on the previous day was sent in by your accounting firm to test your cash policies. Reward the employee's honesty with a small bonus in his or her next paycheck. This is a good way to reward the honest employee and also to announce, diplomatically, that there is a mechanism in place to monitor cash as well as other types of transactions.

This small bonus may be the best money the organization has ever expended, because the entire staff has been made aware there are checks in place!

Cash Register Issues

If a clerk wants to skim money from a cash register, the least obvious way is to ring up a NO SALE transaction, take money from a customer, put it in the cash register, and remove it later.

The most effective way to discourage this practice is to have someone other than the cash register clerk close out the register at unpredictable times. When you are balancing cash receipts with cash register data, an overage rather than a shortage is cause for concern, because it may mean that an employee has taken money from customers and recorded a NO SALE transaction, intending to remove the money later.

Warning signs:

1. If the register has the type of display that can be rotated and the display is not visible to the customer, it makes it easier for the clerk to ring a NO SALE transaction, place the money in the register, and remove it later.

2. Be suspicious if loose coins are on or near the cash register. A clerk recording NO SALE transactions and placing the cash in the register has to keep track of how much was placed in the register so that the proper amount can be removed later. One manner of keeping track is by using loose change; for example, pennies represent dollars to be removed, nickels represent five dollar bills to be removed, dimes represent ten dollar bills to be removed, and so on.

Insurance Committees

As in the case of internal audits, an Insurance Committee is not an option for a very small company. These businesses are best served by seeking advice from a reputable insurance agent.

The purpose of an Insurance Committee is to assess the company's exposure in virtually every area of operation and to determine if the coverage is adequate. This process is very important if the company is serious about risk reduction. Typically, insurance coverage would include, but not be limited to:

1. Fidelity Bond (Employee Dishonesty)

2. General Liability

3. Officers' and Directors' Liability

4. Automobile

5. Errors and Omissions

6. Umbrella

7. Health

8. Life

9. Key Man

Whether the company is large enough to benefit from an Insurance Committee or simply relies on the advice of a competent insurance agent, insurance coverage should be reviewed in depth every year to protect the assets of the company.

With regard to fraud, the most important aspect of an annual insurance review is to study the provisions of the Fidelity Bond and have a predetermined understanding of the procedures the insurer requires in the event of a claim, such as:

1. Does the policy require the insurer to be advised of a possible claim within a certain time period?

2. Does the police department have to be notified within a certain time period?

3. Is a police report required?

The purpose of having this predetermined procedure is to ensure that the company does not inadvertently violate the requirements of the policy, possibly delaying or even eliminating a claim.

Computer File Backups

All computer records, particularly accounting detail, should be backed up daily and stored offsite. Easy to do electronically, this is probably one of the most important protections you can have.

Where's the Fire?

I was retained to study a company's system of internal controls. Something just didn't seem right to management, and they didn't know what was going on. I was brought in to spend a few days to figure it all out. I had some hunches, but decided to reserve judgment until I had the proof I needed.

Late one night, I was awakened by a call from my client. Someone had started a fire in the computer room. The fire department saved the building, but the computer was destroyed. And there were no backup records. Piecing together the accounting records was impossible. Other valuable data, such as email lists and inventory records, were also destroyed and reconstruction would take months. Without the facts, no one will ever know the real story.

Take a lesson from me. While this is not technically an internal control issue, it is closely related. So I urge you to have your information technology manager back up all computer records daily and store them off-site.

Check and Wire Transfer Signatures

Requiring two signatures for every check and wire transfer is a must.

Why? With this policy in place, collusion is necessary to process a fraudulent transaction. Additionally, if a fraudulent check is processed and two signatures are required, there is a strong possibility that one of the signatures is a forgery, which is relatively easy to trace.

Also, the second signature means that another pair of eyes is looking at each transaction, so the possibility of detecting honest mistakes such as duplicate payments, incorrect amounts, or so forth, is enhanced.

Treat your transfers in the same manner that you would your checking account. The same procedures apply and will help you stave off problems in the long run.

Sample Policy On Check and Wire Transfer Signatures

In order to employ the strongest internal controls possible, the company has a policy that requires two signatures on every check processed or wire transfer requested.

The procedure for check requests and wire transfer requests is as follows:

➤ An authorized employee submits a Check Request or Wire Transfer Request.
➤ The request must be approved by the chief executive officer.
➤ The request is processed by accounting.
➤ Two other authorized signers will sign the check or wire transfer.

Employee Name _____

Signature _____

Date _____

Inventory Issues

Unfortunately, many companies do a physical inventory only at the end of the year. If there has been any inventory "shrinkage," it will be too late to investigate the matter and take corrective action. Inventory pilferage can really add up. With that in mind, periodic inventory valuations throughout the year are essential.

Although time-consuming, inventory checks are not difficult. The following are some suggestions that my clients have found helpful:

1. At least one of the inventory valuations should be a surprise and conducted at an unexpected time—for example, the middle of the month or after hours.

2. An occasional "secret shopper" can test certain internal control policies related to dealing with customers purchasing merchandise.

3. Just counting the items in inventory during a valuation is not sufficient. You should actually open a random selection of boxes containing inventoried items. It is possible that a customer could place an expensive item in an inexpensive package. Or an employee, after hours, could switch expensive items with less expensive ones and have an accomplice, acting as a customer, pay for the less expensive item when checking out.

4. If possible, have the items in inventory sealed in clear plastic. This not only prevents soiling, but it also makes switching items much more difficult. In lieu of this, seal boxes with inexpensive prefabricated aluminum foil or heavy-duty clear tape.

Company Credit Cards

Strict policies should be enforced with regard to employee credit cards. All employees must submit the credit card detail with any transaction record. Most companies only require the summary transaction record, which only lists the total amount. In those cases, management really has no idea what the employee purchased.

One of the most common occurrences is an employee getting around a policy that doesn't reimburse for alcoholic beverages. If the employee just submits the transaction summary, alcoholic beverages could have been purchased and no one would know. On the other hand, the credit card detail of the purchase is itemized.

Credit card statements should always be mailed to the CEO off-site. The CEO should review the credit card transactions and investigate unusual ones.

Credit cards can be more than an annoyance; they can be a real liability. They get lost. Card abuse is common. They can get stolen. And an employee who is leaving the organization can rack up substantial personal expenditures. These charges are easy to detect, but not easy to collect.

Consider getting out of the employee credit card business. Most companies are beginning to do just that. Employees can use their personal credit card for business expenses. Of course, your business should be prepared to reimburse employees quickly, especially for big-ticket items or expenses. In addition, if an employee purchases office equipment or furnishings, you should request all backup information. That would include, among other things, warranties and repair information.

Although there are some considerations and inconveniences when employees do not have a corporate card, eliminating them will significantly reduce the risk associated with credit card use and abuse.

Lines of Credit

Two authorized signatures should be required to activate a line of credit. One should be that of the company's CEO (or that person's designee). The other should be the company's CFO, who would normally be the one initiating the letter of credit advance.

This policy reduces the possibility of abuse and protects everyone involved, particularly the CEO and CFO.

You should also require a written authorization for the line of credit request. Use the form shown, and keep it in a separate binder for easy reference and referral.

Letter of Credit Activation Form

A request for a Letter of Credit advance in the amount of $_____

Requested from_____ (Financial Institution) _____

The purpose for activation of this credit line is:_____

Requested by:

Name _____

Title_____

Date _____

Approved by:

Name _____

Title_____

Signature _____

Date _____

Second approval by:

Name _____

Title_____

Signature _____

Date _____

Bad Debt Policy

Customer A sells golf equipment and buys an ad in your organization's magazine for $1,000. An employee of your organization (let's call him B) has account receivable write-off authority; he is also a friend of Customer A. Every company experiences a certain degree of bad debt write-offs. Customers go bankrupt, reorganize, get seriously in debt, or die. A policy addressing write-off procedures is imperative. Why? Because it is very easy for a knowledgeable individual to arrange for "side deals."

On the side, Employee B and Customer A agree that, in exchange for a $500 golf bag, Employee B will arrange to write off the accounts receivable and cancel the advertising debt. Employee B could simply charge the accounts receivable against the Allowance for Bad Debt account. If he were even cleverer, he could charge an expense line item or reduce a revenue account by the debt amount. This would make his actions much more difficult to trace, particularly if the organization is not audited by a CPA firm.

To avoid this type of situation, a formal Bad Debt Policy should be established that includes the following provisions:

➤ Accounting personnel should never have the authority to cancel debt.

➤ A Write-Off of Bad Debt form should be completed, signed by the appropriate individuals, and retained for audit trail purposes.

➤ The CEO, or that person's designee, should personally approve all write-offs.

➤ Finance implements the write-off only after procedures have been followed and signatures acquired.

➤ Records should be maintained of all vendors whose debt has been canceled. Prohibit future dealings until the debt has been paid.

Write-Off of Bad Debt Form

Vendor _____

Address _____

Invoice No (s). _____ _____

Amount due $ _____

Reason for cancellation of indebtedness: _____

_____

Requested by _____

Approved by _____

Internal Audits

Very small companies would have difficulty justifying the necessity for an Internal Audit Committee, but nonprofit organizations with an active board of directors and a sizable employee base should give it serious consideration. The last thing you need is surprises at year-end. An Internal Audit Committee can provide nonprofits with that necessary additional level of internal control throughout the year.

Even if an independent CPA firm audits your nonprofit organization, your board of directors ultimately has fiduciary accountability for the organization. By creating an Internal Audit Committee, you provide your board with another level of assurance that the organization's financial affairs are being managed effectively. This is especially true because an Internal Audit Committee is typically chaired by your treasurer, and that gives the board direct representation. The treasurer is privy to virtually everything that is going on financially within the organization.

Once established, the committee begins to work with the CPA to formulate an Internal Audit Plan that will specify, in detail, the committee's responsibilities. At a minimum, the committee should be responsible for the following:

➤ Have cut-off bank statements mailed directly to the treasurer in advance of the audit.
➤ Review the prior month's bank reconciliation in detail.
➤ Ensure that the organization's internal control policies are effective and, more importantly, being followed.
➤ Meet with representatives of your bank to review signature cards, to ensure that all signers are authorized and that there are no unauthorized accounts.
➤ Meet with your insurance agent to ascertain that coverage is adequate for all policies, with particular attention to the Fidelity Bond.
➤ Test the payroll by comparing payroll records to personnel files.
➤ Contact each employee directly to ensure that there are no "ghosts on the payroll."
➤ Interview all employees who are responsible for receiving and disbursing checks, to ensure that policies and controls are adequate and being followed.
➤ Test disbursements to ensure that invoices have ben approved for payment properly.
➤ Check the accounts payable files and physically contact new vendors to ensure that they exist.

As part of the ongoing procedure, the committee and the CPA should meet to discuss the management letter. The committee is responsible for preparing a report for the board that addresses all of the issues noted in the management letter. This report must also include the status of the resolution of each of the issues.

The internal audit should be scheduled between the last day of the CPA's field work and the date the CPA is expected to begin the next audit—"the window of opportunity"—because it is the period when most fraud occurs. It is also important to conduct an *unannounced* audit. That way, anything unusual in the finances will show up.

At the conclusion of the audit, the committee will prepare an in-depth report of their findings. The formal internal audit report should be reviewed with the chief executive officer and chief financial officer at the conclusion of the audit. In addition, the audit committee report should be shared with the board and the independent CPA firm.

In these times of concern about any organization's financial management, an Internal Audit Committee is relatively easy to put in place, but will create tremendous rewards in the long run. It is one good way to have financial peace of mind.

Stop Payment Orders

It may seem very academic, but you should always check current banking regulations for stopping payments on checks, debit memoranda, and wire transfers. Stopping payments can only be done for legitimate reasons. Doing so for improper reasons, such as simply delaying payments, may be a crime.

If, because of a stolen or lost check, a Stop Payment order is necessary, it is best to follow the method recommended by the American Institute of CPAs and the American Institute of Banking:

1. Make detailed notes covering the circumstances surrounding the reasons for the Stop Payment and what action was taken.

2. Complete a Stop Payment request form and process the Stop Payment order immediately.

3. Safeguard all documentation received from the bank. Maintaining this information (which includes dates and original signatures) could be very important in the event the bank fails to stop payment when advised.

Stop Payment Request Form

Date _____

Check # _____   Check date _____

Amount of transaction $ _____

Reason for stopping payment:_____

_____

_____

_____

Requested by _____

Title _____

Approved by_____

Title _____

Voiding Checks

When a check needs to be voided, you should always follow the five simple guidelines established and approved by the American Institute of CPAs and the American Institute of Banking:

1. Complete a Voided Check form.

2. Write the word VOID, in permanent ink, across the front of the check.

3. Cut off the signature line. This doesn't allow room for a microencoded check amount and ensures that the bank won't accept the check.

4. Mark the back of the check, in permanent ink, with the words: VOIDED CHECK, DO NOT DEPOSIT.

5. Start a Voided Check file that includes:

   ➤ The original voided check

   ➤ A completed and signed Voided Check form

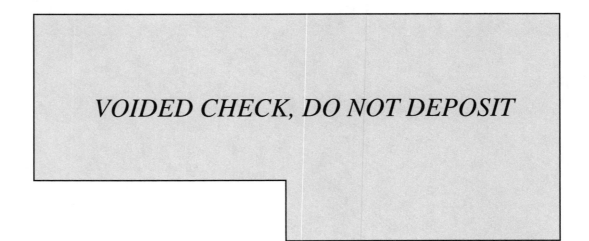

Voided Check Form

Date _____

Check # _____   Check date _____

Amount of check $ _____

Reason for voiding check: _____

_____

_____

_____

_____

Requested by _____

Title _____

Date _____

Approved by_____

Title _____

Date _____

Numbered Check Request Forms

It is advisable for all CEOs of any company to personally sign a Check Request form for all disbursements.

The purpose of the form is to ensure that the CEO is aware of disbursements. But it also serves as a mechanism for the CEO to become familiar with vendors, or question unusual transactions before the actual check is prepared and mailed.

In addition to improving internal controls, Check Request forms provide a good audit trail for each transaction. For added security, invest in an accounts payable software program that requires a check request number before the physical check can be printed.

Check Request Form
No. 4733

Date _____

Requested by _____

Amount $ _____

Make check payable to _____

Purchase order number _____

Details of purchase: _____

_____

_____

Authorized by _____

Signature _____

Expense Accounts

A simple way to divert funds is to embellish, or "pad," travel reimbursement or expense accounts. It is often difficult to monitor these expenses because there is no real audit trail. Consequently, it is imperative that you institute a solid, written policy regarding what you consider appropriate, reimbursable travel expenses and expense accounts.

Expense Account Allowances

One viable option is to grant expense account allowances to select employees. A monthly allowance requires much less paperwork, and it's a predictable, controllable cost. The burden is on the employee to maintain proper records, and that frees up company personnel from handling those tasks.

But there are possible income tax ramifications to handling expense accounts in this manner. To properly adhere to the tax law, employees are required to track and account for expenses paid. If they fail to do so, the expense account allowance is considered taxable income to the employee.

The best way to avoid this is to have the employees complete a monthly form detailing their expenses and provide receipts for actual expenses paid. At the end of the calendar year, if the amount of excess expense account allowance exceeds $600, the employer is required to issue a Form 1099 to the employee for the excess, and the employee is required to claim it as income. Monthly reporting allows you, and the employee, to monitor the amount expended and make the necessary accommodations before year-end.

Travel Reimbursements

If you don't want to pay falsified or improper travel expenses, it's imperative to have strict policies and monitor these policies closely. Without an audit trail, it is realistically very difficult to control travel reimbursement requests. By instituting some of these ideas, you will be a long way toward doing so.

Per Diems   To eliminate tedious bookkeeping that comes from monitoring meal expenses, give employees a fixed amount per day (per diem) for meals. The easiest way to arrive at that amount is to find out the predetermined meal allowance stated by the federal government for each city. Then give that meal allowance to the employee in the form of a travel advance.

Assume that the per diem meal allowance for a city is $40 per day. If the employee will be in that city for three days, the travel advance for meals for the trip would be $120. If the employee spends more than $120, he or she will have to pay the difference. If the employee spends less, he or she can keep the difference. In either case, there is no additional record keeping involved. Receipts are not required under a per diem arrangement.

Food-Only Reimbursements   All employees are required to substantiate meal expenses with receipts, if they are on business. Your organization should have a "food-only, no alcohol" reimbursement policy. Require employees to submit a detailed restaurant receipt for reimbursement, including the credit card charge summary. That way, all expenses are revealed and unauthorized purchases can't be hidden.

Common Carrier Fares   One of the easiest ways to overstate air fares occurs when an employee uses a travel agency to arrange trips. All that is needed is for the employee to get an itinerary from the travel agency for a trip with an expensive carrier and submit that itinerary for reimbursement. Then, without your knowledge, the same employee goes to a different agency to purchase a ticket with a discounted carrier or uses a free frequent flier ticket.

It's not difficult to guess who pockets the difference at your expense. Unless you take on the task of arranging for the tickets and paying the fare directly, the only way to control this situation is to reimburse these expenses with the original airline receipt that is always issued with the ticket. An itinerary or a boarding pass would be unacceptable.

Predetermined Travel Budget   When you plan to reimburse consultants, speakers, or others, you can control costs by negotiating an all-inclusive fee that covers travel expenses. For example, assume that a company negotiates with a consultant to travel from City A to City B for a period of five days for an all-inclusive travel reimbursement of $2,000. In this case, the company simply records the entire fee as a line item travel expense and sends the consultant a 1099 for the $2,000. This method requires far less paperwork because the traveler has the responsibility to keep the receipts and tally the account for the travel expenses on his or her own tax return.

Expenses without Receipts   Whenever possible, always require original receipts for all expenses. For those expenses that typically do not have receipts (such as tips, mileage, and so forth), you need to make policy decisions about the level of the expense you will accept. In these cases, you will be relying on the honesty of your employee. Fortunately, these expenses are usually easy to spot, and the risk of loss to you is small.

CPA Management Letters

Your auditing CPA firm is not hired to uncover fraud. If they should do so coincidently, that's all well and good. But, ferreting out fraud and embezzlement is not their function.

First and foremost, they are hired to issue an opinion on the financial statements. However, during the course of audit field work (particularly while they are studying the system of internal control), it is very likely that your CPA will notice areas of concern. If these areas are significant and reach the level of a reportable condition, the CPA is required to advise the board of directors in the form of a Management Letter.[1]

Auditors are not clairvoyant. It is perfectly acceptable, and even recommended, that the CEO discuss internal control issues of concern with the auditor. As the head of your organization, you should be privy to the contents of the Management Letter before it is reviewed with your board of directors. You never want to be blindsided by a negative Management Letter at a board meeting.

By way of example, let's assume that the auditor discovers poor internal controls regarding bank statement processing. At present, bank statements are sent directly to the CFO, who is also a check signer. Only one signature is required on a check, which makes this a very dangerous combination.

Is the CPA required to report this situation in the Management Letter? Yes. Does it reflect poorly on the CEO? Definitely! Is there anything you can do? Absolutely! Correct the problem!

Since the poor internal controls existed during the year under audit, the CPA is still required to advise your board of directors. However, instead of using language that implies poor management, the wording would now appear as follows: "During the course of the study of internal controls, a weakness was detected in the areas of bank statement security and check signers. However, we are pleased to report that management has taken action to correct the deficiency."

The CPA has advised the board of a reportable condition, but, at the same time, the CEO is in control and is very proactive in the eyes of the board.

Your CPA should discuss the Management Letter issues directly with the board when the financial statements are presented. For the protection of everyone involved, particularly you and your CFO, this discussion should be very straightforward. Remember, the CPA works for the board of directors. Your auditors work through you and your CFO, but they work for the board. Be aware of the issues they raise to the board, so you will be able to correct them quickly.

An effective Management Letter addresses the issues bluntly and, where possible, offers suggestions for improvement. Document any changes you would like to implement, and ask your CPA to include those as part of the Management Letter. All CPAs will work with you to improve controls. Today, it has become a matter of course. Due to increased responsibilities placed on them to prevent fraud, CPAs will even go as far as to threaten an organization with a Qualified Audit Opinion, if there are inadequate internal controls.

---

[1] Management Letters are not restricted to internal control issues, and routinely reflect unrelated areas of concern such as tax issues and the like. Due to the nature of this book, only the internal control aspect of the Management Letter is addressed.

Random Disbursement Checks

In the course of auditing your company, your independent CPA should verify disbursement transactions as follows:

1. Record the number of checks written during the year under audit (the check population).

2. Visually examine each check, looking for unusual amounts, strange vendors, or suspicious checking endorsements.

3. Statistically determine the number of checks (sample of the population) that must undergo thorough auditing procedures. If the sample passes all audit checks, the auditor can assume that the population of checks would also meet auditing standards.

4. Via a computer program, enter the beginning and ending check numbers, to provide random numbers that encompass the sample.

5. Apply required audit procedures to the random sample:

   ➤ Obtain original signatures of all check signers for the audit file.
   ➤ Determine that check request procedures and approvals have been followed.
   ➤ Ensure that the sample check numbers appear on the bank statements.
   ➤ Make sure the amounts of the checks match the amounts on the bank statements.
   ➤ Match the signature on the check with the original signature in the audit file.
   ➤ Match the check number, payee, and amount against the check register.
   ➤ Audit supporting documentation (such as invoices and statements) to check for required approvals.
   ➤ Determine that new vendors physically exist by making phone calls or checking addresses.
   ➤ Examine the endorsement stamp to ensure that the check was endorsed by the intended payee.
   ➤ Compare endorsement stamps for the same payees with other checks.
   ➤ Examine the bank clearinghouse stamps.
   ➤ Check that the bank's microencoded check amount matches the check amount.
   ➤ Perform additional auditing procedures for checks where the bank has made an encoding error.

To close up the window of opportunity for fraud, the CEO should conduct a modified version of these audit procedures on a monthly basis:

1. Have accounting provide the beginning and ending check numbers for all checks written during the month.

2. Check that the beginning check numbers follow the ending check numbers for the prior month, and investigate any unaccounted-for checks.

3. Follow auditing procedures the CPA applied to the sample.

4. Request all supporting documentation, particularly invoices and statements, for the check selected.

5. Always thoroughly investigate new vendors to ensure that they exist.

6. Check all unusual or large transactions.

Because most thefts occur between the time the auditor completes the work at the end of one auditing year and the beginning of the next year's audit, the practicality of doing routine examinations of disbursements during this period is inarguable.

CHECK 21

In 2004, the United States Congress passed a law titled CHECK 21.

Background

The passage of CHECK 21 was a direct result of the September 11, 2001, tragedy. Prior to the passage of the law, original checks cashed by payees were sent from the payee's bank to the originator's bank and eventually included in the payee's bank statement. For example, if a business located in California remitted a check to someone in New York, the New York bank had to physically transport the original check back to California after having presented the check for payment.

After September 11, however, airplanes were grounded for an extensive period of time, effectively paralyzing the entire financial network of the United States.

To ensure that this would not occur again, CHECK 21 was passed.

CHECK 21

CHECK 21 is a system whereby cashed checks are not physically transferred from the receiving bank to the originating bank; instead, an *image* of the check is transferred electronically. Important: This check image is considered the legal equivalent of the original check and as such can be entered into evidence during court proceedings and so forth.

Check Images

Depending on the originating bank, account holders will now receive one of the following:

1. A simple bank statement with no checks or check images enclosed. Usually these banks have check images available online.

2. A bank statement that includes images of only the fronts of checks.

3. A bank statement that includes images of the fronts and backs of checks.

Internal Control Issues

Generally, businesses should always arrange to get images of both the fronts and backs of checks included with their bank statements, even if they are charged a bank service fee. Why? Endorsement comparison is an essential audit tool, and to be precluded from examining backs of checks would prevent auditors from:

1. Determining if employees are signing checks over to third parties.

2. Determining where employees are cashing checks.

3. Ensuring that a vendor's endorsement stamp is consistent and that no one has opened an account in another bank under the same name.

Note: Items 1 and 2 may be indications of "ghosts" on the payroll or employees with financial difficulties.

4

Clever Examples of Embezzlement

Payroll Tax Deposits

YOU MUST CHECK your payroll tax deposits on a periodic basis to make sure they are accurate. Why? Simple. If you don't know how payroll tax deposits work and don't have deposits audited periodically, you are asking for trouble.

A Taxing Example

A local nonprofit seemed to have effective internal controls. Bank statements were mailed to the CEO's home. The CEO reviewed all the checks that cleared the bank and the bank statement. The bookkeeper was not authorized to sign checks. So far, so good.

With only four employees, it was easy for the bookkeeper to prepare the payroll checks weekly. She presented them every Friday morning for the CEO's signature. The payroll checks were always perfectly accurate, so the CEO signed them and personally passed them out to the staff.

Simultaneously, the bookkeeper prepared a check request for the federal payroll tax deposit, which included Social Security, Medicare, and Income Tax Withheld.

Check Request for Payroll Tax Deposit

Amount: $1,410.00

Payable to: U.S. Treasury

Description: Payroll Taxes for payroll period covering _____ to _____

Approved by _____

Title _____

Date _____

Later that day, the bookkeeper prepared the federal tax deposit check and gave it to the CEO for signing. The required tax deposit coupon was included with the check.

```
Smart Company                                                    1234
456 Main Street
New York, NY 10019                          Date  MM/DD/YY


     Pay to the
     Order of ____ U.S. Treasury _____  $  | 1,410.00 |


          Fourteen Hundred Ten and no/100 _____  Dollars


     For _____        J. Roosevelt _____

     1:0120030951:        ||"0878010i'"8"||   1239
```

When the CEO received the bank statement and canceled checks, he saw that the check had been deposited by the IRS and had cleared the bank. Assuming that all the effective controls were in place, the CEO had no reason to suspect that a major embezzlement was taking place right under his nose.

How? The tax deposit amounts were wrong. Since no one was checking the tax deposits for accuracy, there was a simple, but effective, embezzlement opportunity. The bookkeeper made an intentional overpayment in the amount of $300 on every tax deposit check. That meant that every week an overpayment of $300 was sent to the IRS.

At the end of every quarter, the bookkeeper prepared the Form 941 federal payroll tax return, as well as the state returns. The CEO signed the returns personally, but never had the returns checked for accuracy.

At the end of the year, the bookkeeper prepared the W-2 forms and, once again, the CEO never had the W-2s checked for accuracy.

The bookkeeper simply recorded the weekly overpayments as federal income tax withheld on the payroll tax returns. She noted the $15,600 total weekly overpayments as federal income tax withheld on *her own personal W-2 form*. When she filed her personal Form 1040 income tax return, she received a personal income tax refund check in the amount of—you guessed it—$15,600.

When the dust settled, it was discovered that the bookkeeper had been doing this for 25 years!

How It All Unraveled

Interested in knowing how the embezzlement was discovered?

This scheme ran for 25 years, resulting in a combined total of almost $400,000. It wasn't discovered until the bookkeeper got greedy.

The offending employee retired on August 17, and was owed $25.00 for expenses she paid on behalf of the organization. She prepared a check request for reimbursement, and her boss approved it. She later prepared a handwritten check payable to herself, and her boss signed it accordingly.

```
                                                        #3456
                                                        8/17/yy
  Pay to    Retiring Employee                          $25.00

  The Sum  Twenty-five and no/100              Dollars


                                    A. Boss
```

She took the check to the bank later that day, endorsed it, and prepared a deposit slip. Unknown to anyone, she wrote the check out with a pen with erasable ink and she erased the amounts.

```
                                                        #3456
                                                        8/17/yy
  Pay to    Retiring Employee                          $

  The Sum                                      Dollars


                                    A. Boss
```

She now had a check payable to her signed by her boss with no amount written. Incredibly, she altered the check to $35,000 and deposited it into her account!

```
                                                        #3456
                                                        8/17/yy
  Pay to    Retiring Employee                          $35,000.00

  The Sum  Thirty-five thousand and no/100     Dollars


                                    A. Boss
```

The significance of the 17th of the month was that she knew the bank's cut-off date for mailing the bank account was always the 15th of every month. She had almost a full month to cover her tracks.

Altering a handwritten check is easy, but preventable if certain basic controls are in place such as:

1. Using a bank's Positive Pay service. The bank's computer would have detected that the amount was changed and would not have honored the check when presented.

2. Although old-fashioned, check imprinters still work. A check imprinter is an inexpensive piece of equipment available at any office supply store. Simply dial in the amount, insert the check and pull the lever. The check will be imprinted with THE SUM $25.00 in blue and red ink, and the check will also be perforated, preventing altering.

3. Handwritten checks should be written with a gel pen rather than an ink pen. A knowledgeable person could tape over the signature and dip the check into a common household liquid that would eradicate the ink, and then dry the check with a hair dryer. Once it is dried, a perpetrator could make the check out to whomever he wants and for any amount! Always use a gel pen instead of an ink pen for handwritten checks.

Discovering the $35,000 altered check was easy. It simply appeared in the bank statement a few weeks later. When the altered check was found, I was called in to check any other occurrences. One of the first areas I audited was payroll. The random tax deposit indicated a $300 tax overpayment, which prompted me to research more tax payments. It was odd that all of them had the $300 overpayment. I traced the overpayments to the federal income tax withheld on the quarterly Form 941 payroll tax return and, eventually, to the federal income tax withheld on the bookkeeper's personal W-2. Voilà!

If the bookkeeper had not altered the $35,000 check, the payroll tax scam would probably never have been detected.

More importantly, this situation could have been avoided if the CEO had arranged for a periodic check of the payroll tax deposits and tax returns. Additionally, this serves as a good example of what can happen if a company doesn't have an annual audit by a CPA firm. The board of directors felt that they didn't have the budget, and that there was no need for an audit. So, to save the $5,000 annual audit fee, they lost $15,600 every year for 25 years. That's why I always tell my clients that it is better to be safe than sorry.

A Clever Variation

A business owner meets with a customer who gives him a $2,500 check as a deposit on an item.

On the way to the office, the owner stops at the bank and deposits the check personally. He asks the bank to copy the check for him and gives the check copy and deposit slip to the staff accountant. The accountant takes the information from the owner and pockets the $2,500!

How is this possible?

Simple. If the accountant had handled the transaction properly, she would have increased cash and credited a revenue on a deposit account. However, she instead increased cash properly but credited the state withholding tax liability account, and sent the $2,500 in with the next state withholding tax deposit. She then included the $2,500 as additional state withholding taxes on her personal W-2 and received the money in the form of a state withholding tax refund.

Check Switching

Make sure that someone other than a finance employee reviews bank statements. As previously stated, at a minimum bank statements should be mailed to the CEO's home for review. For larger organizations, however, having copies of bank statements, with the corresponding canceled checks, sent to a secured Post Office box accessible only to the CEO or members of the internal audit team for review is unquestionably *the* most important internal control for businesses of any size. This allows the CEO or auditors the opportunity to examine each individual check and review any suspicious transactions.

Sound overzealous? It's not. With computerization, it's simple to replace checks that are issued for legitimate purposes with phony ones. An unsuspecting CEO (and even an experienced auditing CPA) would never know the difference. The importance of the CEO reviewing bank statements and checks became apparent during the course of my very first fraud examination.

Experience Is the Best Teacher

As a course instructor, I was asked to spend some time reviewing basic internal controls for a class of CEOs. I had no actual fraud examination experience at the time, so I dusted off an old auditing textbook for some suggestions. One piece of advice stood out from all the others.

The next day, I told my class that all CEOs should have their company's bank statements mailed off-site. They should then take the responsibility for reviewing the statement and all the cleared checks, before sending them on to accounting for bank reconciliation purposes. Little did I know that this advice would initiate my career as a fraud examiner. Note: After reviewing Section 6 of this manual, "Identity Theft," I feel that it is actually much safer to have the copies of the bank statements mailed to a Post Office box rather than someone's home, unless the individual's personal mail box is secured.

One CEO in the class took my suggestion seriously. She went to the bank after class to change the name and address on the statement, from the staff accountant's name at the office to her name at her home address. Wisely, she decided not to mention that she had changed the procedure to anyone, particularly the staff controller.

The following week, she received the first bank statement at her home. Not dreaming that embezzlement was taking place, she was shocked when she saw that check 1234, made payable to, and endorsed by, the staff controller, had cleared for $2,000. And, to make matters worse, someone had forged the CEO's signature on the check. Clearly something was wrong, and she wisely did not confront the controller at this point.

Since I was the one who had given her the advice about reviewing the statements, the CEO decided to call me to help her investigate the situation. Over the next few weeks, we jointly uncovered a brilliant embezzlement scheme that had earned the controller in excess of a half-million dollars and that launched my career as a fraud investigator.

What We Did

It was obvious that something was seriously wrong, but neither of us had any idea what. I decided to examine the accounting backup for the check 1234 by reviewing the check register. The check register records indicated that the check was payable in the correct amount of $2,000, but the office records showed the payee as the U.S. Postal Service! Looking further into the situation, I found that the actual accounting records verified that there was an approved check request for the postage check in the files, and an actual postal receipt was stapled to the check request.

We then went to the bank. We decided that the best course of action was to copy the front and back of the canceled check payable to the controller and put the original check back in the bank statement. At our request, the bank changed the address on the statement back to the controller's name at the company's address and remailed it immediately. Clever, huh?

Two weeks later, I went back to the company. I went to the file cabinet where the bank statements were stored and found the statement that the bank had resent two weeks earlier. Opening the statement, I discovered that check 1234 had been removed and replaced with another check (also 1234) for the same amount. The substitute check was payable to the U.S. Postal Service, and even had a post office cancellation stamp on the back, showing that it had been cashed by the post office.

It was clear that the scam involved the post office. To further investigate, I reviewed all bank statements for the prior three months. I made copies of every check that cleared the bank through the post office (all of which appeared perfectly legitimate). We then got copies of the bank's copies of these checks. Several of the bank's copies were payable to the controller, while the office copies were payable to the U.S. Postal Service!

How It Was Done

When the controller was confronted, she confessed to the embezzlement and told us how she did it. Brilliantly, she was able to fool both management and a very competent, experienced independent CPA firm that audited the company's records.

She ordered a supply of checks from a check printer. Then she went back to the check printer several weeks later and told them that a temporary agency had cleaned the office and, by mistake, had thrown out the printed checks. She reordered a new supply of checks that were identical to the first set; same color, same account number and, most importantly, same check numbers.

As you probably suspect, she kept the first set of checks in the office and the second set of checks at her home. The organization wrote a lot of checks for postage, including checks for the postage meter, the bulk mail account, media mail, the business reply account, and so forth. The office policy stated that the CEO had to sign each check request and each corresponding check. The controller was not authorized to sign checks.

One day, the controller presented the CEO with a routine check request for $2,000 for postage, which the CEO approved.

> CHECK REQUEST
> Date:MM/DD/YY
> Amount: $2,000.00
> Payable to: U.S. Postmaster
> CEO Approval: G. Lincoln

After getting approval, the controller wrote the check and presented it to the CEO for her signature.

Smart Company		1234
456 Main Street	Date MM/DD/YY	
New York, NY 10019		

Pay to the
Order of _____ U.S. Postal Service _____ $ | 2,000.00

_____ Two thousand and no/100 _____ Dollars
Grand Bank & Trust Co.
New York, NY

For _____ G. Lincoln _____

⑆0120030951⑆   ⑈"0878010I"8"⑈   1239

The controller now had the approved check request and the signed check in her possession. She put the signed check in her purse. She took the diskette out of the office computer and took it home with her. That evening she inserted the diskette into her home computer, where she had installed the same check-processing software. Using the duplicate set of checks, she scrolled up, on her display, to check 1234:

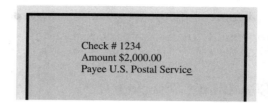

She placed the cursor at the end of the payee's name and erased the U.S. Postal Service as the payee, leaving the payee line blank:

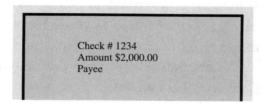

Then, she simply typed in her own name as the payee:

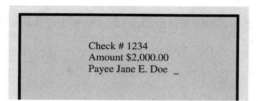

She hit the Print key and printed the check:

Smart Company
456 Main Street
New York, NY 10019   Date MM/DD/YY   1234

Pay to the
Order of ____ Jane E. Doe _____ $ 2,000.00

_____ Two thousand and no/100 _____   Dollars
Grand Bank & Trust Co.
   New York, NY

For _____   G. Lincoln

I:0120030951: ||"0878010l"'8"|| 1234

Then she did the simplest thing in the world. She forged the CEO's signature. Please remember that it is physically impossible for banks to match checks presented for payment against original signature cards. Banks process millions of checks every day, so comparing checks against signature cards is a physical impossibility. It is the businesses's responsibility to ensure that checks are signed properly, not the bank's.

She endorsed the check and cashed it at a bank other than the company's bank, which made it more difficult to detect the forged signature. This simple scheme, performed repeatedly over the years, resulted in a gain to her of over $500,000.

Why the CPA Didn't Discover It

The controller was an experienced accountant who knew what the CEO did, and did not, review. She also knew the CPA firm's auditing procedures, and she had the control of the bank statements—a dangerous combination.

She knew that CPAs are hired to catch inconsistencies and discrepancies in financial reporting. They are hired to verify that the financial statements are accurate. They are *not* hired to check for falsification or to catch fraud. She was well aware that a CPA's checklist of audit procedures, with regard to auditing disbursements, would involve these activities:

1. Review check request approval procedures, check signing authority, and other procedures, to ensure that they are followed.

2. Witness individuals signing checks with their signatures for the audit file.

3. Follow Generally Accepted Auditing Standards to ensure that a large enough sample of checks is audited statistically.

4. Make sure that the audit samples (randomly selected checks) correspond to those on the bank statements by number and amount.

5. Look for proper check endorsements.

6. Verify that the check is backed up with a valid receipt.

7. Check to see that bank clearinghouse stamps appear on the backs of the audit sample.

8. Make sure that the bank's microencoded amount on the bottom front of the check (after the preprinted account number, ABA routing number, and check number) matches the written check amount.

The falsified check 1234 ended up in the audit sample. After a thorough review, the auditors concluded that the check was genuine because:

1. A check request was signed by the CEO.

2. The approval signature matched the CEO's original signature in the audit file.

3. Check 1234, for the correct amount, appeared on the bank statement detail.

4. The CEO's signature on the check itself appeared authentic.

5. The check was endorsed by the post office.

6. There was an authentic postal receipt in the file.

7. The back of the check also was affixed with the bank clearinghouse stamps.

8. The check had the correct microencoded amount of $2,000.

```
Smart Company                                    1234
456 Main Street
New York, NY 10019
                                       Date   MM/DD/YY

Pay to the
  Order of   U.S. Postal Service                   $2,000.00

Two thousand and no/100                            Dollars
Grand Bank & Trust Co.
    New York, Ny

For                                    G. Lincoln

1:0130030451:      11'03750101"8'11    1234      200 000
```

How Was All This Possible?

The mysteries were unraveled as I completed the investigation.

How did she encode the checks? The answer lies in how the bank corrected erroneous coding of checks. They taped a piece of white tape, with the correct amount over the incorrect amount. All the controller had to do was find an old check with the correction tape, remove the tape from the old check and tape it on the bottom of the fraudulent check. Of course, she had to find an old corrected check with the proper amount first, so it took some sorting time for her to make her scheme work.

And how did she get clearinghouse stamps on the checks? Simple. The controller went to a rubber stamp supplier and had them made. They looked exactly like authentic clearinghouse stamps, and they fooled everyone, including the auditors.

How did she make all this work through the U.S. Post Office? One word—collusion. A postal employee simply endorsed the back of the fraudulent check with the actual postal endorsement stamp! No auditor in the world could catch this because the endorsement stamp *was* the postal endorsement stamp.

With regard to a receipt, the postal employee simply recorded a $2,000 transaction, producing a receipt given to the thief, and then voided the transaction, resulting in no traceable sale at the post office.

And, finally, how did she get away with it for so long without getting caught? It's really quite simple. The controller knew the system, and that system was within her control. She was an experienced, well-qualified, and apparently loyal employee.

The CEO had a great deal of faith in her abilities and gave the controller even more responsibilities. This led to the CEO giving up a great deal of control. Under many circumstances, this would be fine. But if there is a lurking embezzler in your finance office, it could spell trouble. And finally, why didn't this excess postage look suspicious on the internal financial statements? Simple. When the controller concocted the scheme years ago, she started at a mere $100, but over time she gradually raised the amount to $2,000. In the interim, since the controller was in effect the budget coordinator, she literally was able to budget in the annual embezzlement, so the internal financial statement appeared to be in line.

The End Result

With the overwhelming evidence, the CEO confronted the controller and pressed charges. The controller, as well as the post office accomplice, received prison terms.
Case closed.

Ghosts on the Payroll and Ghost Vendors

Ghost Employees

If the right controls are not in place, it is relatively easy to place a nonexistent or unauthorized person on a payroll and pocket the money. As long as the perpetrator is not greedy, this scam can go undetected for long periods of time.

Ghosts are typically put on the payroll by someone who actually prepares the payroll, or by the manager of satellite offices who has the authority to hire people and can simply forward fraudulent employment documentation to the parent office for processing.

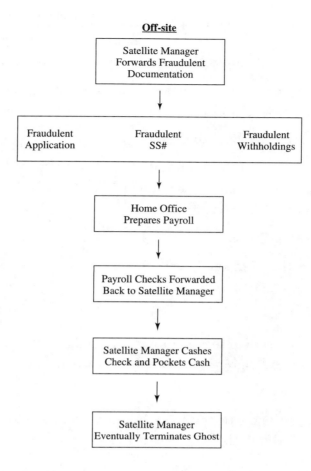

Off-site

Satellite Manager
Forwards Fraudulent
Documentation

Fraudulent   Fraudulent   Fraudulent
Application   SS#   Withholdings

Home Office
Prepares Payroll

Payroll Checks Forwarded
Back to Satellite Manager

Satellite Manager Cashes
Check and Pockets Cash

Satellite Manager
Eventually Terminates Ghost

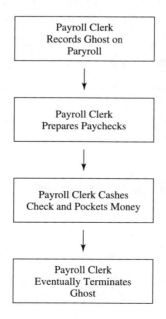

Payroll Department

Payroll Clerk
Records Ghost on
Paryroll

Payroll Clerk
Prepares Paychecks

Payroll Clerk Cashes
Check and Pockets Money

Payroll Clerk
Eventually Terminates
Ghost

Steps to take to prevent ghosts on the payroll:

1. **Employment Application**

   Ensure that the organization's employment application is thorough and that the "employee" fills it out completely and no spaces are left blank.

2. **Social Security Number Check**

   Always request the applicant's Social Security card and follow that up with an independent check of the number. There are databases that enable employers to check on Social Security numbers.

3. **Reference Check**

   Ensure that someone checks the personal and professional references noted on the employment application.

4. **Credit Check**

   Make sure that the employment application states that the employer has reserved the right to run a credit check of the applicant.

5. **Time Sheets**

   Time sheets are not popular, but they are practical. Ensure that time sheets are signed by both the employee *and* the supervisor.

6. **Direct Deposit of Payroll**

   Seriously consider requiring employees to participate in Payroll Direct Deposit. As noted in the warning signs that follow, often ghost employees do not deposit payroll checks into bank accounts, lessening the probability of detection. One aspect of Direct Deposit of Payroll is that the employee is *required* to have the net check deposited into a bank account, making a ghost employee scheme somewhat more difficult.

7. **Distribution of Payroll Checks or Deposit Receipts**

   If possible, payroll checks or deposit receipts should be distributed to employees by someone other than the person who prepared the payroll or the off-site satellite manager.

8. **Independent Check of Employees**

   At least once a year, have the payroll checks or deposit receipts distributed by the organization's CPA or a member of the Internal Audit Committee, to prove the existence of all employees. This should be done at a time between the auditors' conclusion of audit field work for one year and their return to start field work for the next year. See "The Embezzler's 'Window of Opportunity'" in Section 1 of this manual.

Obviously, a clever person in the right position can circumvent the checks noted. However, there are a few patterns and warning signs of potential ghosts on the payroll.

Warning Signs

1. Remember that the individual who has placed a ghost on the payroll has done so for the purpose of stealing the net paycheck. Therefore, the perpetrator will arrange to have the net paycheck as high as possible, by:

   ➤ Having little or no federal or state income taxes withheld by claiming a high number of dependents on Form W-4.

   ➤ Having no voluntary deductions for insurance, savings bonds, charitable contributions, and so forth.

2. The ghost on the payroll is almost always a part-time employee, because full-time employment complicates things by triggering such things as health insurance applications, life insurance applications, disability insurance applications, and so forth.

3. The ghost on the payroll is almost always employed and terminated during the course of one calendar year, lessening the chance discovery by auditors. They are "rehired" after the auditors have completed their field work. (See "The Embezzler's 'Window of Opportunity'," in Section 1 of this handbook.)

4. Checks made payable to ghosts on the payroll are usually not deposited into a bank account, lessening the probability of detection. Look at the back of payroll checks—checks that are cashed at check-cashing services or liquor stores, or signed over to a third party, or the like are *always* suspicious.

5. The surnames of ghosts on the payroll are frequently very common names such as Smith, Jones, or Miller, lessening the chances of name recognition detection.

6. Employment applications for ghosts rarely note a spouse.

7. Employment applications for ghosts often don't list an actual address, but rather list a post office box address or a nonexistent address.

8. Employment applications for ghosts rarely note a land-line telephone number, but rather note cellular telephone numbers that are easily terminated and hard to trace.

9. Employment applications for ghosts often don't note prior employers but rather note "stay at home dad" or other excuses to account for employment absences.

A Little Humor   Fraud is a serious problem, of course, but occasionally there are instances of humor.

This really happened.

A car dealership employed over 100 people. The business was not audited, and the payroll clerk was virtually unsupervised, a dangerous combination.

It seems the payroll clerk had her husband, who was in a building trade, fraudulently on the payroll as a part-time employee for *fourteen years!* (It would be easy to hide a part-time employee for a business of this size.)

How was the husband ghost detected?

It seems the husband accepted a job in another state, and his wife went with him. The husband, not knowing how the system works, *filed for state unemployment!* Of course the state sent an employment verification to the business, and this is how the ghost was discovered.

Ghost Vendors

A deterrent to being victimized by a ghost vendor scheme is to have a thorough, current, and updated Approved Vendor File. At a minimum, vendor information on file should include:

➤ Full legal name of vendor
➤ Street address
➤ Contact name
➤ Business telephone number
➤ Fax number
➤ Email address
➤ Website address
➤ Federal Identification Number (FIN)

As in the case of ghosts on the payroll, perpetrating a ghost vendor scheme usually requires the perpetrator to be in an upper-level position or in the finance department. A ghost vendor scheme is relatively simple:

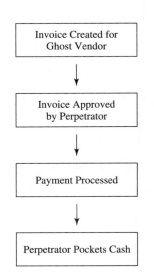

A deterrent to a ghost vendor scheme is to have the independent auditors validate the existence of new vendors the organization has been doing business with since the conclusion of the previous fiscal year.

Verifying the existence of new vendors is relatively easy:

1. Physically visit the new vendor's offices.

2. Contact Dun & Bradstreet for business data.

3. Research corporate records.

4. Research public databases.

5. Check with the bank where the checks have been deposited.

6. If the vendor's invoice notes a PO box address, inquire at the post office as to the owner of the box.

Warning Signs

1. As in the case of ghosts on the payroll, perpetrators of ghost vendor schemes almost always arrange for fraudulent payments between the times the auditors conclude audit field work for the prior year and start audit field work for the subsequent year. (See "The Embezzler's 'Window of Opportunity'," in Section 1 of this handbook.)

2. Usually, phony invoices for ghost vendors have a post office box remittance address rather than a street address.

3. Attempts to call the ghost vendor usually reach an answering machine.

4. Often, invoices from ghost vendors do not include information typically included on legitimate vendor invoices such as:

   ➤ FAX numbers
   ➤ Email addresses
   ➤ Website addresses

5. Sometimes originators of phony invoices use consecutive or very close invoice numbers.

Tip: A simple but hard to detect ghost vendor scam is to first prepare a check payable to an approved vendor and later prepare a check for the same invoice with a clever variation of the approved vendor's name. For example:

Approved vendor name: ABC Service *Corp.*
Variation: ABC Service *Co.*

The best way to avoid this type of ghost vendor scheme is to randomly compare endorsement stamps on the back of checks looking for variations, different account numbers, and the like.

The Danger of Acronyms

Any entity that you do business with should be instructed to make its checks payable to the full legal name of your company. Even if your company is widely known by its acronym, actively discourage your customers, or members, from making checks payable to it.

The best way to learn that lesson is by example. Here it is.

For years now, the American Crayon Association has referred to itself as ACA. Therefore, its customers and members routinely make checks payable to the acronym. The accounting clerk receives the checks, gives the customers or members credit in the accounting records, prepares the deposit, and takes the deposit to the bank.

Pretty straightforward and foolproof. Right? Wrong. This can result in a serious problem.

Let's just assume for a moment that the accounting clerk needs cash for a personal matter. So he comes up with a scheme. He goes to a bank in a nearby city, presents the proper paperwork, and opens up an account under the name Acme Creative Advertising, another ACA. The clerk then deposits some of the checks payable to ACA into his new account.

He can hide the stolen payments any number of ways. He can take the ordered product from inventory and mail it out personally. Or he can pretend that the checks are a bad debt and write the money off existing accounts receivable. As long as the clerk doesn't get too greedy or careless, no one will know the difference.

This activity is very difficult to detect. Beware and be wise—follow these suggestions:

1. Use your bank's Lockbox Service. Employees don't come into contact with checks mailed to the company, so diversion of these checks is virtually impossible.

2. Request that customers and members make their checks payable to your company's full legal name.

3. Your endorsement stamp should appear as follows:

```
FOR DEPOSIT ONLY
YOUR COMPANY NAME
(e.g., American Crayon Association, Inc.)
```

4. The stamp should include the full legal name of your organization, but *not* your bank name and account number. Any dishonest person could draft a check payable to your company, and then pick up your bank name and account number when their check is cashed. The embezzler could then have fraudulent checks printed with that information microencoded on them.

5. Note that the endorsement stamp includes "Inc." I strongly recommend using "Inc." because someone can easily divert a check by depositing it into an account under the name American Crayon Association, LLP. So use your full legal name. It's safer.

6. Endorse the back of checks as soon as possible after receipt.

7. Make sure endorsed checks are only delivered to accounting. If the department responsible for the sale needs the check for verification, it can be given copies.

As is the case with having checks written to your acronym, processing checks payable to a vendor's acronym is also risky. If, for example, your company incurs a legitimate debt in the amount of $10,000 to the Allied Business Corporation (also known as ABC), your payment of that debt could be in jeopardy. All an embezzler has to do is intercept the check, deposit it into an account in another bank for, let's say, the Associated Building Council (another ABC). Then, when the funds become available, the embezzler just draws down the account.

You will lose out on two counts. You won't find out about the misappropriation until it's too late to track it down. Therefore, recovering your money will be virtually impossible. And your vendor still has an existing balance. Even though you have just fallen victim to a theft, you still have an obligation to satisfy the original debt.

So, to avoid this type of misappropriation, make sure all checks include the vendor's full name (with its legal distinction) and the street address. In addition, always check your mailroom security.

Bank Account Reconciliations

Not only should CEOs receive bank statements off-site and review them, they should also see all statement reconciliations.

The following scenario will show you how easy it is to perpetrate a fraud, if the bank reconciliations are not routinely reviewed. And it can happen even if your business is audited by an independent CPA firm.

It's December. The company operates on a calendar year. An invoice for a legitimate printing bill is approved for payment and sent to the CEO with a Check Request form. The CEO forwards the documentation to the finance department for check preparation. A check for $5,000 is prepared, signed by the CEO (plus a cosigner), and mailed to the EZ Printing Company, which cashes the check.

On the sly, the company accountant processes another check for the same invoice in a different check run. This check is put in the safe and not mailed.

In come the auditing CPAs. If they discover the second check, they will bring it to the attention of the accountant. Of course, he's prepared with an excuse. It's the last month of the fiscal year. Everyone is busy with the budget, preparing payroll tax returns, typing W-2s, and so forth. This was just a simple mistake. So he retrieves the check from the safe and voids it.

If the auditors don't catch the intentional duplicate payment, the second check will appear on the December bank reconciliation as an outstanding check. All the accountant has to do is be patient, wait for the CPAs to finish their audit file work, and issue the financial statements. Once this is over, the accountant can forge the check signers' signatures and cash the second check payable to the EZ Printing Company by opening up an account in another bank under that name.

The probability of the auditors discovering this is very slim. The original check was outstanding on the December bank reconciliation, which had already been audited by the CPAs. They wouldn't spend much time on a previously audited year-ending bank statement.

This type of scam is very difficult to stop. The perpetrator has a believable, built-in excuse if the double payment is caught. The only sure way to uncover it is for the CEO to check the bank reconciliations. Any unauthorized outstanding checks would stand out like a sore thumb. It's well worth your time and effort.

Wire Transfers

Meeting with your bank on a regular basis is just good business. It's the best way to ensure that your company is receiving the optimal bank service. It also gives you the opportunity to check the bank's records regarding your authorized wire transfer signers (as well as authorized check signers). You might be in for a surprise.

A Coast-to-Coast Horror Story

A not-for-profit organization applied for, and was awarded, a sizable grant from the state in excess of two million dollars (if you can't relate to a grant, insert Letter of Credit or something similar). The CEO signed the grant contract, and the funds were then available to be drawn down. When the grant was awarded, the staff accountant told the CEO that he had no grant accounting experience and was uncomfortable with that responsibility. The CEO thanked him for his honesty and advertised for a new CFO. Two weeks later they offered the job to a qualified applicant who accepted the position. The CFO was not a check signer nor an authorized wire transfer agent.

A few months later, after gaining the confidence of the CEO and staff, the CFO told the CEO that bank examiners were having the bank contact certain customers to update their bank records, and the organization was required to file new check signature cards and wire transfer agreements. The documents presented to the CEO noted the authorized signers' names and titles and, once again, the CFO was not an authorized signer.

```
+-----------------------------------------------------------+
|                  Wire Transfer Agreement                  |
|                                                           |
|        Name             Title            Signature        |
|                                                           |
|    P. Leahy         President       _____     |
|    J. Crowley       Treasurer       _____     |
|    H. Stuhldreyer   Vice President  _____     |
|    _____     _____    _____     |
|    _____     _____    _____     |
|                                                           |
|              Corporate Secretary _____     |
+-----------------------------------------------------------+
```

Seemingly, this was just a routine bank request, so the CEO signed the document, along with the other approved signers—the corporate treasurer and the vice president. With the addition of the signature of the corporate secretary (as required by the bank) and the imprint of the corporate seal, the paperwork was complete. But not the scheme.

After getting the required signatures, the CFO then simply typed in *his name* and title and signed the document. The bank wasn't updating its records; the CFO told his bank contact that the organization was updating *its* records. Because he appeared to have authority, the bank gave him the documents. The CFO was now an authorized check signer and wire transfer agent, only no one knew it!

```
+-----------------------------------------------------------+
|                  Wire Transfer Agreement                  |
|                                                           |
|        Name             Title            Signature        |
|                                                           |
|    P. Leahy         President       P. Leahy              |
|    J. Crowley       Treasurer       J. Crowley            |
|    H. Stuhldreyer   Vice President  H. Stuhldreyer        |
|    C. Smith         CFO             C. Smith              |
|    _____     _____    _____     |
|                                                           |
|              Corporate Secretary  J. Jackson              |
+-----------------------------------------------------------+
```

The CFO then proceeded to make legitimate wire transfers through one particular bank employee, and over the next few months they developed a natural business friendship.

Then, one Friday afternoon, at exactly 1:45 PM Mountain Time, just before the bank closed (any transactions after 2:00 PM would be recorded the following Monday), the CFO entered the very busy bank lobby. He gave his "favorite" bank employee a sizable wire transfer to a bank in California that, once processed, would virtually wipe out the organization. At exactly 1:45 PM Pacific Time, his partner in crime in California transferred the money out of the country—approximately 1.5 million dollars.

The scheme surfaced the following week, but it was too late. And, the situation went from bad to worse.

The organization filed a claim with the insurance company that handled its Fidelity Bond. They discovered that the bond excluded officers and directors. After retaining an attorney to prove that the CFO wasn't technically an officer, because he didn't have a vote on the board of directors, they were finally able to negotiate that hurdle.

Then, they discovered that the bond coverage was only for $500,000. Unfortunately, the embezzler stole over 1.5 million dollars.

And it didn't end there. When the state was advised of the missing grant funds, they decided to sue the CEO and the individual board members personally for reimbursement, because they had the legal basis to do so. The grant contract stipulated that the organization had to carry a Fidelity Bond for the full amount of the grant, and the organization hadn't bothered to check on it.

And finally, if the situation seems as though it couldn't get any worse, it did. There was no resolution in spite of the thorough investigation following the incident. No one can uncover the true identity of the perpetrator. Everyone knows it was the CFO, but his documents and personnel file were completely made up! This incident was a setup from the moment the individual applied for the position. In the end, they will never be able to find the perpetrator for prosecution.

A Word to the Wise

To protect yourself, the board, and the company, employ the services of a knowledgeable attorney to review every contract before it is signed. Periodically, visit the bank to check the bank's records and the current signature authorizations. If you receive bank documents that require signatures, cross out blank spaces with a marker so no additional names can be added. And, routinely review the adequacy of, and exclusions to, your Fidelity Bond. You have it for your protection, but, as is the case with any insurance policy, it needs to be reviewed and amended periodically to be of value to you and the organization. And finally, always perform a complete background check on any individual who will be employed in your accounting area. When all is said and done, you never know whom to trust with your company's money.

Postage Issues

The way the world is today, we have to look at every situation as a potential hazard. That even includes the relationship your company has with your local post office.

I know what you are thinking. If you can't trust the U.S. Postal Service, whom can you trust? Well, probably no one, when it comes to your finances.

A Bad Working Relationship

There was a CFO who perpetrated an elaborate check-switching scam that involved a second set of checks and an accomplice who worked at the post office (see "Check Switching," in this section). Even with other procedures in place (such as having the bank statement mailed to the CEO off-site, a proper endorsement stamp, and a visual check that there was no tape over the encoded area indicating a bank error), the perpetrator was still able to get away with the scam—with a little help from his friend.

In another example, an accounting clerk went to the post office and purchased a postal money order with a check from his company. This eliminated the need for an elaborate check-switching operation, or a postal worker accomplice. The check would clear the bank with a proper endorsement stamp and bank clearinghouse information. The microencoded amount would be authentic. Life couldn't get any easier for the embezzler.

The Trouble with the Mail Today

You also have to worry about what is happening in your own mailroom. While playing golf at a famous resort, one CEO arranged to have his picture taken with a client, as a gift.

To expedite delivery of the present, he wrote a note and hand-addressed an envelope, asking the mailroom clerk to run it through the postage meter. The CEO picked up the print later that day, put it in the prepared envelope, and dropped it off at the local post office. As he was putting it in the mail slot, he noticed that the clerk had metered the envelope for $37.00 instead of $37¢.

When he asked the post office clerk what could be done, he was told to turn in the postage meter tape on the envelope, and he would get a refund of $37.00 less a 10% handling fee. His pleasure at receiving the $36.30 refund changed to displeasure when he learned that his mailroom employee was getting refunds on a routine basis. Let's just call this "Post Office Petty Cash."

To prevent postal abuse, you will need to institute tight procedures that are reviewed by someone knowledgeable in postal abuses. At the very least, you should have an arrangement, in writing, with your postmaster that no one in the company is allowed to purchase postal money orders with company checks or obtain refunds for overpayments. When they do occur, the refunds should be credited to your account.

Kiting

Did you realize that if you arrange for periodic deposit audits, you will take the appropriate measure to prevent check kiting? In a very simplistic example, here's how a kiting scheme works:

Day One   An organization receives receipts totaling $20,000.

Receipts are entrusted to the finance department, which enters the deposit accurately in the accounting records.

A dishonest accountant, however, doesn't take the deposit to the bank on the following business day. Instead, he or she pockets the receipts.

Day Two   Receipts total $25,000.

Once again, the accountant pockets the $25,000.

Day Three   Receipts total $22,000.

The accountant uses $20,000 out of the third day's receipts to cover the $20,000 deposit for the first day. He or she keeps the extra $2,000 as a "slush fund" to balance subsequent deposits.

Day Four   Receipts total $25,000.

The accountant applies this total, plus $2,000 from the slush fund, to cover the second day's deposit of $25,000.

End of the Month   At the end of the month, the accountant pockets the total receipts from the last two business days of the month. This time, he or she records these receipts as "deposits in transit" on the bank reconciliation.

The accountant prepares the internal financial statements. The statements have been misstated by kiting deposits (covering them with subsequent deposits) and showing the last two days' receipts as outstanding items. At this point, the accountant has absconded with four days' worth of receipts.

This system of combining kiting of receipts and phantom deposits in transit is very difficult to detect. It is extremely difficult to reconstruct, particularly if it is done over a long period of time, and the organization is not audited.

An Ounce of Prevention

➤ Utilize a bank's Lockbox Service. Kiting receipts and falsifying deposits in transit on the bank reconciliation is virtually impossible with a Lockbox Service, because employees never come into contact with original receipts.

➤ Have an audit conducted by a competent CPA firm. In the course of an audit, the CPA will perform a "proof of cash" auditing technique that is designed to expose kiting and improper deposits in transit.

➤ Have the CPA firm come in, unannounced, during the middle of the year to do a thorough audit of an interim period. It is also important to arrange for a cut-off bank statement.

➤ Have the receipt clerk's responsibilities assumed by another employee on his Management Day off.

Manual Checks (Handwritten and Typed)

Handwritten or typed checks are vulnerable to alteration of the check amounts.

Computer-generated checks protect the amounts by imprinting a series of dollar signs to the left of the check amount so that additional numbers cannot be added. The words spelling out the amount of the check start on the far left of the line and end on the far right, so that words cannot be added. This protection is not afforded in any other check-writing method.

The Case of the Retiring Bookkeeper

A trusted bookkeeper was planning to retire in a year. Her husband had retired a year before, and started a retirement business called The Paper Clip Delivery Service. They lived in a rural Texas town. Every two weeks, he drove to Houston, where he was able to get favorable prices for his clients from a national office supply store that didn't deliver to this town. As payment for his services, he received a $25 service fee from his clients. One of his clients (as it turns out, his only one) was his wife's employer.

The bookkeeper told her boss that they needed to transfer $35,000 from an interest-bearing account to their disbursing account, which was a routine occurrence. The CEO signed the transfer slip. Unbeknownst to the CEO, the bookkeeper kept the signed transfer slip, but didn't make the transfer.

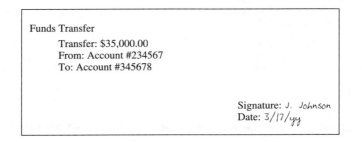

Months went by, and the bookkeeper's retirement date was approaching. After her retirement luncheon, she told the CEO that she and her husband were moving to Oklahoma. She asked if he would approve a check for the $25 delivery fee owed to her husband. The CEO signed the check request, she prepared a handwritten check accordingly, and the CEO signed it. After leaving the office for the last time, the bookkeeper made two stops that afternoon.

```
                                                        6789

Pay to    Paper Clip Delivery Service                $25.00

The Sum  Twenty-five and no/100                      Dollars


                                    J. Johnson
```

First Stop, Her Company's Bank   At the bank, the bookkeeper went to the center island and removed the funds transfer slip from her purse. It was dated 3/17/yy. This day's date was August 17, so she simply changed the three to an eight, and she then transferred the $35,000 to the disbursing account.

Second Stop, Her Husband's Bank   She then drove to the bank where her husband's Paper Clip Delivery Service account was held. Unknown to anyone, when she had made out the handwritten check, she used erasable ink! She erased the amounts and then had in her hands a blank, signed check:

```
                                                        6789

Pay to    Paper Clip Delivery Service                $

The Sum                                              Dollars


                                    J. Johnson
```

Unbelievably, she marked the check up to $35,000!

```
                                                        7894

Pay to    Paper Clip Delivery Service                $35,000.00

The Sum  Thirty-five thousand and no/100             Dollars


                                    J. Johnson
```

She knew that the bank's cut-off date for bank statements was the 15th of the month. By doing the fraudulent transaction on the 17th, she knew that the altered check wouldn't be discovered for a month. She returned to the bank a week later, when the funds had been transferred and the altered check had cleared the banking system. She closed out the account and pocketed the $35,000.

Tip   If it is necessary to hand-write a check, always use a gel pen rather than an ink pen. Another common trick is to put tape over a check signature, dip the check in a common household liquid that erases all but the printer's ink, and then blow-dry the check. The thief now has a signed check with no payee or amounts. The solvent eradicates ink, but not gel.

The Case of the Petty Cash Fund

A trusted staff accountant was also the petty cash agent (not uncommon in most small businesses). At the end of each month, he typed up a check to himself for $100 to replenish the fund, and presented the check to the CEO for his signature.

	7894
Pay to _____ Donald Miller _____	$100.00
The Sum _____ One hundred & no/100 _____ Dollars	
	E. Layden

After hours, alone in the office, the accountant put the check back into the type-writer and lined up the striker across from the number 1. He hit the backspace key and typed in a comma. He then hit the key twice and typed in a 0. And finally, he pressed it twice again and typed a 1, changing the numbered amount from $100.00 to $10,100.00. A hefty petty cash fund.

To complete the transaction, he lined up the striker across from the letter O, hit the backspace key the appropriate number of times, and typed in two words: Ten Thousand.

With that simple action, he was now in possession of a typed check, signed by the CEO, and payable to himself for $10,100.00.

	7894
Pay to _____ Donald Millar _____	$10,100.00
The Sum _ Ten Thousand One hundred & no/100 _ Dollars	
	E. Layden

He deposited the check in an out-of-state bank. He did this for ten consecutive months. Since the bank statements were mailed directly to him, he knew that no one would be aware of the altered checks, and he simply falsified the financial statements he prepared.

$101,000 richer, the accountant gave his notice just two weeks before the CPA firm was due in. The theft was discovered, but much too late.

Preventing Check Scams

The altering of the ten petty cash checks took place during the classic embezzler's window of opportunity. This is the time that management has to be alert to potential fraud.

Of course, this scam would have been discovered, or not even attempted, if the CEO reviewed bank statements and canceled checks, off-site. Positive Pay, too, would have prevented these two scams.

And finally, manual checks can be protected if the amounts on the checks are printed with a check protector machine, available at any office supply store. This simple machine imprints the words THE SUM and the dollar amount on the appropriate line in blue and red ink, and perforates the paper.

Auditing Receipts

It is very important to arrange for a thorough audit of an entire month's receipts to verify that the proper accounts have been credited. And this should be done at least once a year.

Let's assume that you institute an internal control practice that requires that your office manager, administrative assistant, or receptionist endorse all checks received, complete a deposit slip, and maintain a log of those checks (as an audit trail) before sending them to finance.

One deposit includes a $1,000 check payable to the company. The checks and deposit slips are sent to finance, which processes them and physically deposits them at the bank (including the $1,000 check), which clears the bank routinely.

Sounds fine, except that the finance director credited the $1,000 check to the Federal Income Tax Withheld account, instead of the proper one. The $1,000 is now considered withheld income tax on the finance director's personal return. At the end of the year, she simply adds the $1,000 to the actual amount withheld on her personal W-2. She has given herself a "bonus" of $1,000 in the form of a personal IRS income tax refund check.

The original check was never tampered with. It was simply credited to the Federal Income Tax Withheld account, instead of a revenue account. To prevent this type of embezzlement, you should arrange for a thorough audit of an entire month's receipts, to ensure that every check received has been credited to the proper account—especially, during the embezzler's window of opportunity, the time between one year's audit and the one in the following year.

5

Steps to Take If You Have Been Victimized by Fraud

Documenting a Fraud Action Plan

OBVIOUSLY, NO ONE wants to be the victim of a fraud scheme, but possible victimization is a reality all organizations face. A prudent business practice is to have a preplanned and well-thought-out strategy of action to take if fraud is suspected. A draft of such a plan follows:

1. **Never ever accuse anyone of an impropriety—get the facts.**

   Remember that you may be wrong, and if you are, there is a probability you will be on the wrong end of a defamation lawsuit. Be patient and thoroughly investigate the situation before any action is taken.

2. **Contact an employment law attorney.**

   If you suspect fraud, get advice on how to proceed, from a competent employment law attorney familiar with your state and federal employment law. This is a very important step in avoiding any associated legal issues concerning termination for fraud.

3. **Contact your independent CPA.**

   Inform your independent CPA firm that fraud is suspected and inquire if they are competent in the areas of fraud investigation, forensic accounting, and so forth. If they don't feel comfortable in this area, ask them to recommend a CPA firm that is experienced in this area.

   Once you have contacted the right CPA firm, they will assist you with the investigation, help with any insurance claims, prepare for going to trial if necessary, and handle other important areas suggested in this plan of action.

4. **Work from copies.**

   When you initially contact your independent CPA firm, they will tell you the importance of protecting the evidence and working from copies of original documents related to the incident.

   Place the original documents in a safe deposit box or safe location that the offender does not have access to. Remember that copies of documents are often not admissible as evidence in court, and if original documents are lost, stolen, or altered, a valuable aspect of your criminal case, insurance claims, and the like may be compromised.

5. **Take detailed, copious notes.**

   Again, when you initially contact your independent CPA, you will be told of the importance of taking detailed and thorough notes of everything related to the incident.

   Realistically, it may be *years* before going to trial after the incident is discovered, and anything can happen in the meantime: an understandable loss of memory, people retiring, people resigning, and so forth. When detailed notes are taken, a full record of the incident will be available to another employee, attorneys, CPAs, and the like.

6. **Read your Fidelity Bond!**

   After review, note important provisions of your bond in this plan of action, such as police report requirements, required time frame to file a claim with the insurance company, and so forth.

7. **Review the Conditions of Employment agreement.**

   This is always an uncomfortable situation, but the stress may be relieved somewhat if the employee was required to sign the important Conditions of Employment agreement whereby the employee has acknowledged that he or she understands what to expect in the event of a fraud investigation.

   Note: Please reference and read thoroughly "Conditions of Employment Agreement," in Section 3 of this manual.

   Steps 8 through 16 are concerned with actually confronting the alleged perpetrator and are included in the agreement.

8. **Do not discuss the situation in the employee's office, cubicle, or other work area.**

   Never have this discussion in the employee's office, but rather in an executive's office, conference room, library, or another neutral location. Remember that the offender's office almost assuredly contains vital evidence related to the incident.

Never allow an offender access to this evidence because it will be important to forensic accountants, attorneys, police detectives, insurance company, and so forth.

9. **Always have a witness.**

At a minimum, the termination discussion should *always* include a witness selected by management, regardless of the nature of the situation. This witness is of particular importance in the event of any form of male-versus-female confrontation. If a man finds it necessary to confront a woman, the witness should always be another woman. Conversely, if a woman has to confront a man, the witness should be another man.

Obviously, the purpose of the male/female confrontation witness is to avoid any allegations of sexual impropriety and for physical protection of the woman.

It's possible that other witnesses may be required, such as your attorney, CPA, or other persons essential to the case.

10. **Protect yourself and other employees.**

It is a sad commentary on our society, but realistically, violence in the workplace is common.

If there is even a *hint* that this is a possibility, contact your local police department for advice. Often they will either send a uniformed officer to sit in on the discussion or allow off-duty officers to provide this service for a fee. Regardless, the police department will be prepared to offer advice as to how to proceed.

11. **Change computer passwords!**

While the discussion is taking place, have an Information Technology (IT) representative void the suspect's computer passwords and address any other important IT issues such as email access and so forth. Failure to do this could result in the suspected offender's accessing the system off-site, compromising important data, and so forth.

12. **Have the discussion during nonbusiness hours.**

Ensure that the confrontation takes place before or after regular business hours. The purpose of this, of course, is to avoid an unnecessary office scene, embarrassment, and the like.

13. **Ensure surrender of organization property.**

The employee should be required to surrender organization property such as door keys, credit cards and so forth. It may also be necessary to have the locks changed.

14. **Employee should not collect his/her property from the office.**

   Have two employees go to the offender's office to remove important personal effects such as a purse, wallet, car keys, and the like. Two employees should always do this to avoid any accusations of theft of cash.

15. **Escort the perpetrator from the office.**

   Never allow the employee to return to his or her office—remember, the office contains valuable evidence important to the fraud investigation, forensic accountants, and attorneys, and if the employee has access to evidence it could affect the integrity of the case.

16. **Have other employee property gathered by coworkers.**

   Inform the offender that nonessential employee property such as photos will be gathered by two employees, and these items will be couriered to the employee's residence the following business day.

17. **Make notes of the discussion.**

   After the discussion, the executive and the witness should compile detailed notes of the discussion. The notes should include, at a minimum, the following:

   ➤ Date and time of the discussion
   ➤ Names and contact information of the executive, witness, police officers, CPA, attorney, and the like.
   ➤ The offender's physical reactions to questioning
   ➤ Other important information as needed

   The purpose of these notes is to provide detail needed by attorneys and accountants in the event that litigation is necessary.

18. **Get a police report, if necessary.**

   On advice of your attorney, don't neglect to file a police report of the incident, as this report is required of Fidelity Bond claims, forensic accounting data, litigation strategy, and so forth.

19. **Proceed with a Fidelity Bond claim.**

   It is very common for management to take the Fidelity Bond (employee dishonesty insurance) for granted and not know who is included on the bond, the amount of the bond, and actions to take to proceed with a claim.

20. **Prosecute?**

   The perpetrator should be aware that the organization (or the Fidelity Bond carrier) may prosecute the offender in the event of employee dishonesty.

The Conditions of Employment agreement should clearly state that prosecution may lead to a criminal record. Criminal records are public information and discoverable by subsequent employers pursuing background checks on prospective employees, significantly damaging the offender's prospects for employment.

Obviously, the discussion to prosecute would be made on a case-by-case basis, but material dishonesty should always be prosecuted. If there is no prosecution, there is no record, and the offender could perpetrate the scam on an unsuspecting subsequent employer.

21. **Decide how to relate the circumstances of dismissal to others.**

    Get advice of counsel on how to handle relating circumstances of the termination:

    ➤ Internally with staff
    ➤ With inquiring customers and so forth
    ➤ With regard to reference checks by subsequent employers

22. **And when it's all over. . . .**

    Reconstruct the details of the occurrence and change procedures so that it cannot happen again!

Fraud Examinations and Assembling the Fraud Team

A fraud examination is significantly different from an audit, although it is understandable that someone not familiar with the various services offered by a CPA could confuse the two.

An audit of financial statements is very general, and the purpose is for the CPA to express an opinion on the financial statements, hopefully unqualified. Exposing fraud is not the goal of an audit, although occasionally, of course, fraud is discovered during the course of a routine financial audit.

A fraud examination is usually very specific and due to suspicion that fraud may exist or have already occurred. It is very important to assume that a fraud examination will eventually end up in court, so it is essential that detailed and copious notes be prepared as the engagement progresses.

A typical fraud examination consists of the following steps:

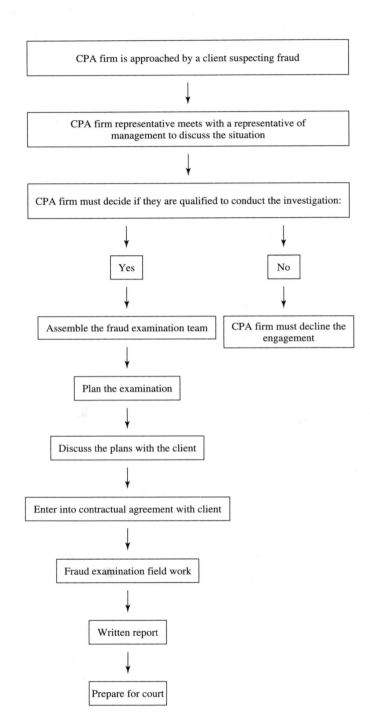

CPA Firm Approached by Client Suspecting Fraud

Typically, the client has already discovered fraud or is suspicious of an internal embezzlement or outside fraud, and their first impulse is to contact their CPA firm for help and guidance.

After this initial contact is made, a meeting should be arranged between representatives of the client and CPA firm.

CPA Firm/Client Meeting

This meeting should take place either at the CPA's office or a neutral location, but never at the client's office, if it is believed the fraud is ongoing, and suspected employees are still on staff.

At this meeting, a full discussion of the suspicious activity takes place, and the two parties reach a conclusion as to whether or not to proceed.

CPA Firm Qualified to Proceed?

The CPA firm representatives must examine their qualifications to proceed. If the fraud examination is beyond their abilities, they have an obligation to decline the engagement and advise the client that it would be in their best interest to select another firm.

Assuming that the CPA firm is satisfied with their qualifications to proceed, the next step would be to assemble the fraud examination team.

Fraud Examination Team

Of course, every fraud is different from the next, so the individuals serving on the team will vary from incident to incident. It is possible that one examination would only require the services of one experienced CPA, while another may be composed of several people.

Possible fraud examination team members may include the following:

➤ Members of the CPA firm
➤ CPAs from other firms experienced with fraud examination
➤ Labor law attorneys
➤ Criminal law attorneys
➤ Outside consultants
➤ Computer and software experts
➤ Private investigators
➤ Client representatives
➤ Others as deemed necessary

Planning the Examination

Once the fraud examination team is assembled, they work out the details of the fraud examination plan based on what is known at the time about the incident. Details, of course, may change once field work is commenced and more information becomes available.

Discussions with Management

The next logical step is for representatives of the CPA firm and management to meet, once again either at the CPA's office or a neutral location, to discuss the following:

- Initial fraud examination plan
- Roles and responsibilities of team members
- Time frames
- Financial arrangements
- Final written report
- Other areas particular to the incident

Contracting with the Client

Obviously, the CPA firm and client should enter into a contract detailing key elements of the fraud examination to avoid misunderstandings, particularly regarding financial arrangements.

Field Work

Depending upon the nature of the incident, elements of field work may vary. Typical field work may consist of the following:

- Cut-off bank statement or online review of cleared checks and the like
- Cut-off credit card statement review
- Collection of evidence
- Inquiries and interviews of key personnel, witnesses, and so forth
- Observations of behavior

Important: As noted, a key element of a fraud examination is the expectation that the incident may go to court. Therefore, adequate documentation of all actions taken, evidence collection, interview results, and so forth is absolutely essential.

Written Report

A written report will be prepared, summarizing the incident, backed up by details gathered during field work. Remember, never accuse anyone of any wrongdoing, and don't hesitate to secure appropriate legal opinion when necessary.

Preparing for Court

Preparing to go to trial dictates that a forensic accountant become involved. For a full discussion on the role of a forensic accountant and preparing for litigation, see "The Basics of Forensic Accounting," next.

In summary, a fraud examination is substantially different from an audit of the financial statements. This work is challenging, always different, and often very rewarding and satisfying, when an engagement is successful.

The Basics of Forensic Accounting

Technically, the term "forensic accounting" means preparing an expert witness accountant for litigation as part of a team representing either the prosecution or defense in a matter relating to a fraudulent activity. Over time, however, the term "forensic accounting" has also become synonymous with investigative accounting procedures. We will now address literal definitions of forensic accounting, that is preparing to go to court, and will explore the steps from selection of a forensic accountant to testimony.

Forensic Accountant vs. Traditional Accountant

As stated previously, a forensic accountant is one prepared to go to trial, while a traditional accountant is one recognized as an authority in the discipline of accounting. Practically all forensic accountants started their careers as traditional accountants in various roles such as bookkeepers, controllers, tax preparers, chief financial officers, independent CPAs, and so forth, because experience in traditional accounting fields is an important qualification for a forensic accountant.

Forensic accountants are commonly relied on in several areas, the most common being:

➤ Divorce settlements
➤ Business valuations
➤ Personal injury
➤ Embezzlement, fraud, identity theft, and falsification of financial statements

Here, we will address only the last bullet point, that being fraud issues.

Forensic Accounting: Education and Training

As stated previously, almost all practicing forensic accountants started their careers as traditional accountants, and therefore their basic educations routinely mirror each other. Basic education typically includes undergraduate study and postgraduate study, and almost all forensic accountants eventually become CPAs, because this credential is a vital component of the expert witness accountant's curriculum vitae, discussed below.

Typically, one desiring to make the transition from traditional accountant to forensic accountant would seek out and work for a CPA firm specializing in this field for invaluable hands-on experience.

Finally, this person typically would join professional organizations recognized in the fraud area, such as the Society of Certified Fraud Examiners, to take advantage of seminars offered on the subject and so forth.

Characteristics of Competent Forensic Accountants

Traditional accountants are often stereotyped as unassuming, conservative, detail-oriented, quiet, and well-educated professionals, and these stereotypes are generally found to be true. Although these traits clearly vary among individuals, a few of these traits would be detrimental to a forensic accountant.

The forensic accountant will be retained as an expert witness during deposition and litigation, and thus experience very tough questioning from opposing counsel in front of jurors. A good forensic accountant has to be thick-skinned and self-confident and have excellent verbal and written communication skills. In other words, a good forensic accountant is viewed as someone more extroverted than a typical traditional accountant.

Building a Curriculum Vitae

Before selecting the expert witness forensic accountant, an attorney will request a curriculum vitae (CV) from each candidate considered. Obviously, the CV that includes better education, experience, professional credentials, articles authored, professional affiliations, and so forth will be given more consideration, so plan to firm it up.

A typical CV includes the following:

➤ Personal information such as name, address, telephone number, email address, and so on
➤ Degrees earned
➤ Professional credentials (Certified Public Accountants (CPA), Certified Fraud Examiner (CFE), etc.)
➤ Continuing professional education
➤ Professional memberships American Institute of Certified Public Accountants (AICPA), state societies of CPAs, American Society of Certified Fraud Examiners (ASCFE), etc.)
➤ Prior expert witness experience
➤ Books and articles authored
➤ Military history
➤ Employment history

The CV should be thorough, but there is a fine line that separates thoroughness from *too* much information, because opposing counsel will try to exploit any weaknesses included. The attorney will give advice on what to include or not include before the CV is provided to opposing counsel.

Finally, ensure that all information included in the CV is truthful and factual, because any erroneous statements will be a major embarrassment and possibly affect the outcome of the trial if discovered by opposing counsel.

Tip: An individual intimidated by speaking in public would not project the air of self-confidence required of a testifying forensic accountant. If that is the case, consider taking public speaking training such as a Dale Carnegie course. Also offer to speak on the subject for your local chamber of commerce or church. In addition to valuable speaking practice, these engagements can legitimately be included on your CV.

Another Tip: Having articles published is an essential aspect of a strong CV, because it establishes the forensic accountant as an expert in the field. Getting an article published isn't nearly as difficult as you might imagine.

➤ First, draft an article on some interesting embezzlement you were involved in uncovering or became aware of.

➤ Second, have your article edited. Rarely can anyone edit his or her own work, and an article that is not professional will not likely be considered for publication.

➤ Third, do your homework. Remember, magazines, newsletters, and newspapers are *looking* for content! Submit your article first to the editor of a local publication that you feel may be interested in your work, and work your way up to larger publications. You'll be surprised how often your work is accepted!

Personal Attributes

The rules of discovery mandate that the CV of the forensic accountant be provided to opposing counsel, so, as stated earlier, it is imperative that all information be truthful. It is equally important that the forensic accountant have high standards of personal integrity and remain cool under pressure from the opposition's lawyer.

In addition to professional information included in the CV, opposing counsel will also investigate the *personal* background of the forensic accountant to discredit his or her testimony during litigation.

Personal information that may be brought up at trial may include:

➤ Academic grades
➤ Current status of license and any lapses
➤ Current status of compliance with Continuing Professional Education requirements
➤ Driving record issues such as a DWI or DUI
➤ Criminal record
➤ Credit record
➤ Employment history
➤ Divorce issues
➤ Substance abuse issues
➤ Bankruptcy
➤ Lawsuits

➤ Liens
➤ Questionable business associates or friends
➤ Relationship with the client or client's associates
➤ Relationship with the client's attorney
➤ Conflicts of interest
➤ Fee arrangements

If a forensic accountant has anything embarrassing in his or her past, it is important that he or she advise the attorney he or she is working with. No one is expecting the forensic accountant to be perfect—just be prepared that it is likely these items may come up at the trial, and get advice from your lawyer about how to respond on the witness stand if they do.

The Team

A typical forensic accounting engagement involves, at a minimum, a team of three:

➤ The attorney
➤ The forensic accountant
➤ Another accountant who will assist the attorney and work behind the scenes

Roles:

Attorney: Obviously, the attorney represents his or her client, plans case strategy, and works with the forensic accountant and accounting assistant.

Forensic Accountant: He or she will eventually appear in court as an expert witness. Remember, the forensic accountant's CV is open to discovery; this person must be cool under pressure from questioning by opposing counsel and is under oath.

Accounting Assistant: This person's background is generally *not* subject to the discovery rules. Therefore, this person typically does the on-site detail work and acts as a technical advisor to the attorney.

The Agreement

To avoid any possible misunderstandings, often the attorney may want a letter of agreement from the forensic accountant. Typically, this agreement includes the following:

➤ Fee arrangement
➤ Scope of work to be performed
➤ Anything unique or important relating to the engagement
➤ Deadlines

Sample Accounting Firm/Attorney Agreement Letter

Date_____

Attorney Name
Firm Name
Street Address
City, State, Zip Code

Dear_____:

This letter is to confirm our conversation with regard to providing forensic accounting services with regard to (case).

Fees for services provided and related expenses will be billed as follows:

Expert Witness: $_____ per hour
Services to be provided:
    Conferences
    Depositions
    Testimony
    Other services as necessary

Senior Accounting Staff: $_____per hour
Services to be provided:
    Conferences
    Data examinations
    Report preparation (if requested)
    Other services as necessary

Clerical Staff: $_____per hour

Expenses:
    Travel
    Photocopying
    Postage/Courier
    Other expenses as necessary

If the terms of this arrangement are acceptable, please sign on the appropriate line, date and return with a retainer fee of $_____.

Sincerely,

Accountant Name
Firm Name

Agreed:

_____
Attorney Name

_____
Date

Field Work

Field work is the actual investigation and information-gathering portion of the incident in preparation for going to trial. A good guideline to consider when planning field work is the requirements included in SAS 99, "Consideration of Fraud in a Financial Statement Audit," (Section 2 of this book) as well as elements included in a fraud audit.

Important elements to consider include:

1. Protection of evidence

   When evidence such as tampered checks, deposit slips, bank statements, and the like are gathered, it is very important to remember to safeguard the original document by placing it in a safe deposit box or other secured location and *work from copies.* Why? It is possible that the document could be lost or stolen, and often copies are not allowed to be submitted as evidence, seriously jeopardizing the case. Safeguarding the evidence also prevents tampering with original documents.

2. Document, document, document!

   Take detailed and copious notes of *everything* related to the investigation, such as:

   ➤ Dates
   ➤ Times
   ➤ Actions taken
   ➤ Discussions held
   ➤ How physical evidence was gathered
   ➤ People interviewed
   ➤ Places visited
   ➤ Observations such as strange behavior
   ➤ Audit trails
   ➤ Witnesses

The importance of adequate documentation cannot be overstated. Besides its obvious importance as evidence at the trial, this detailed documentation would be available and invaluable to a successor forensic accountant in the event that something happened to the original team. Additionally, it can often be *years* between the time field work is concluded and actually going to trial, and it would be understandable to forget details over an extended period of time.

Depositions

After the forensic accountant has been selected, the team gathered, and field work completed, the next phase of the assignment is preparing the forensic accountant for his or her deposition by opposing counsel.

A few points to remember:

➤ The opposing counsel is representing *his or her* client and therefore will do everything in their power to discredit the forensic accountant! Expect it and don't get upset—that's their job.

➤ Be prepared and review deposition strategy with your attorney.

➤ Remember, as noted earlier, it is likely that anything embarrassing about your past will come out during the deposition. Be prepared to respond appropriately as advised by the attorney.

➤ Be honest with your responses, and if you do not know the answer to a question, say so.

➤ The deposition will be in front of a court reporter. The court reporter will forward the written deposition to your lawyer. It is very important to review the written deposition carefully and bring any errors to the attention of your attorney for correction.

The Trial Phase

Okay, everyone has done his or her work to this point, and now we are preparing for the actual testimony of the forensic accountant as the expert witness at the trial.

Your attorney will review the following with you, but this is what you can expect to do:

1. Review all of the data so that you will be prepared.

2. Carefully review the written deposition so that you will not contradict yourself.

3. Discuss testimony strategy with your counsel.

4. Arrive early on the day of the trial.

5. Dress conservatively.

6. Pause before answering questions. Besides giving you more time to think, it allows your attorney time to object.

7. Don't speak to or even make eye contact with jurors.

8. Try to disassociate yourself from questioning, and don't take the questions personally. Remember, you are not on trial.

The Pros and Cons of Forensic Accounting

Pros:

1. **It's emotionally rewarding.**

   It's a nice feeling to know that you are contributing something positive to society by exposing fraud and corruption and helping to protect victimized and innocent people.

2. **It is exciting, challenging, and varied.**

Each individual incident of embezzlement is almost always different from the others, and thus piecing together parts of a complex scenario is usually challenging—requiring thoroughness and ingenuity—but very satisfying when a conclusion is reached.

3. **It can be lucrative.**

Individuals hire forensic accountants because of their experience and, like specialists in any other field, forensic accountants can expect compensation that can be very lucrative.

Cons:

1. **Failure.**

On occasion, people perpetrating fraud are so clever and cunning that coming to a satisfactory conclusion of an investigation is virtually impossible. This of course is very frustrating.

2. **Working within the system.**

Another downside to forensic accounting is accepting the fact that often the dragon slays the knight, or in other words, the perpetrator "beats the system."

It is always frustrating to prove conclusively that an embezzlement took place, only to see the case dismissed due to a technicality.

3. **Opposing attorneys.**

If an engagement goes to court, the forensic accountant will have to face the opposing counsel in both the deposition and testimony phases.

As stated earlier, it is that attorney's job to protect his or her client, and therefore the attorney will do all he or she can to discredit the expert witness not only regarding professional qualifications, but also very personal issues that may be embarrassing. It is difficult not to take these statements personally.

4. **Intimidation.**

Unfortunately, violence in the workplace is a fact of life in our society. While rare, intimidation of a forensic accountant has happened. Remember, desperate people can take desperate action, and take whatever action you deem necessary to protect yourself.

Tip: When planning your career, consider having business cards, letterhead, and the like with a post office address rather than a street address. Why? For the protection of everyone, it may be better that your office address or residence not be known to certain unsavory individuals.

6

Identity Theft

Identity Theft Issues

This actually happened:

Joe and Nancy McVictim enjoyed a very comfortable lifestyle, had a very nice house and an expensive, late model car, and frequented Bud's Place Restaurant almost every Sunday for their brunch. They had no way of knowing, but they were being targeted.

After brunch one Sunday, the identity thief discreetly followed them home. The thief now knew their address. As with most people, their daily routine was predictable, and after a short time, the thief knew when the house was vacant.

On days when no one was home, the thief waited for the mail truck to deliver their mail and leave the neighborhood. The thief then simply drove into the neighborhood and removed the mail from the unsecured mailbox outside their home.

Taking the mail, the thief then opened the envelopes in a manner that no one would notice (microwave oven, freezing, regluing, steaming, etc.), and made *copies* of what he needed:

➤ Bank statements
➤ Credit card bills
➤ Securities statements
➤ Insurance premium invoices
➤ Telephone bills

After making copies, he put the materials back in the envelopes, resealed them, and put the mail back in the mailbox. The McVictims had no idea someone had been tampering with their mail. It took about a month to gather all the information he needed for the scam, including important billing cycles.

One day during this period, the perpetrator did research at the local courthouse and easily found out the maiden name, Carol Williams, of Joe McVictim's mother, often a security question.

One Sunday the McVictims went to their favorite restaurant, and this is when the nightmare started.

Arranging to be directly behind them in the check-out line, the thief watched them pay their check, making a mental note that Mr. McVictim used his "VIP" credit card, and the amount including the tip was $60.00. The McVictims went home, once again having no idea what had just occurred.

This is the telephone call they received about two hours later (the call was made to their *unlisted* number, which the thief got from the telephone bill in their mailbox).

"Hello."

"Is this Nancy McVictim?"

"Yes it is."

"Mrs. McVictim, I'm sorry to call you on a Sunday afternoon, but this is Ken Miller from the VIP credit card company. I have a few questions to ask you, as there is a possibility someone not authorized is using your credit card in Las Vegas. Do you mind?"

At this point Nancy McVictim was understandably concerned.

"Would you mind if I asked you a few questions?"

"No, of course not."

"First, were you or your husband in Las Vegas during the past six days?"

"No, we've been right here."

"For security purposes, is your husband's mother's maiden name Williams?"

"Yes it is."

"And was your last transaction early this afternoon at Bud's Place Restaurant, for a total of $60.00?"

"Yes it was."

Convincing? You bet!

The thief then convinced them that their card was being fraudulently used, that they would have to cancel it and would be receiving a replacement card in the mail.

Shortly thereafter, as noted above, their ordeal started.

A few days later, a bill from their car insurance company arrived. It seems the thief had financed in their name and insured under their automobile insurance policy a *very* expensive late-model car!

As identity thieves know how to do, the thief got a fraudulent state driver's license with:

➢ Joe McVictim's real name

➢ Joe's real address

➢ Joe's real driver's license number

➢ But someone else's picture

(These fake driver's licenses won't fool police officers, but they do fool store clerks, which is the intent.)

Since the thief had all of the bank account information, he simply went to an office supply store and purchased the software with which checks can be printed at home. The replacement checks had Mr. McVictim's real name and address printed on the face of the check, and of course his real checking account number micro-encoded on the bottom front.

Armed with the fake driver's license and checks, the thief completely wiped out Joe's available cash, as well as his $25,000 line of credit on his checking account.

The thief maxed out all of their credit cards.

Not satisfied with the cash available in the checking account and line of credit, the thief went online and transferred sizable sums of cash from the McVictims' savings over to their checking account and even got their savings! The thief managed to figure out Joe McVictim's bank PIN. How? Once again, many of us are predictable, and a clever thief knows that, often, someone's PIN may be a combination of relatively few factors, those being:

➢ Initials

➢ Birthdays

➢ House number

➢ Last four digits of telephone numbers

➢ Last four digits of a Social Security number

Or a PIN may be a very easy to remember number, such as 1234 or 9999.

The experienced thief put these factors into a computer program and eventually discovered the PIN, in this case Joe's initials and birth year (JM57).

Joe and Nancy were hit for over $250,000.

We'll discuss steps to take if you have been victimized shortly. If you follow procedures, your personal liability is small, but the problem is the unbelievable hassle required to recover your funds, including:

➢ Police reports

➢ Completing Affidavits of Theft

➢ Changing all of your bank accounts

➢ Getting new credit cards

➢ Contacting credit bureaus

➢ And even, in the case of the McVictims, changing Social Security numbers!

On a smaller scale:

Do you think it is possible to steal money by *depositing* money into someone else's account? As you probably surmised, yes it is.

Sal Howe was filling out a deposit slip at the bank. The gentleman next to him was also completing a deposit form and talking on his cell phone. Unknown to Sal, the caller had a *picture* phone and took a picture of Sal's deposit slip. The thief now knew Sal's full name, address, and checking account number. The thief also had a picture of Sal's paycheck and knew Sal's employer and the amount of the check; the check stub indicated Sal was paid semimonthly. The thief also took a picture of Sal's signature as he endorsed the check.

The thief, as in the case above, easily procured a fraudulent driver's license with Sal's name, the thief's picture, and a nonexistent address on the other side of town.

The thief went into a branch of the same bank Sal used, on the same side of town as the address on the fake license. Approaching a teller, and armed with identification and Sal's account number, the thief ordered *deposit slips* and had them mailed to a post office box.

Once the deposit slips were printed, the thief started making small cash deposits of around $50 routinely in Sal's account, always managing to get this one particular teller. After about two weeks, the teller was used to the thief making deposits, of course.

The thief then went into the bank, knowing that Sal had probably deposited his paycheck for the end of the month two days earlier. Going to the same teller, the thief asked what the available funds were in his checking account, and of course the teller told him. The thief, stating to the teller that he needed traveler's checks for a vacation he was taking, now simply filled out a cash withdrawal slip and walked out with just under $10,000!

Scary?

There are many, many variations of these instances of identity theft, but everyone is a potential target, so everyone should take precautions as well as have a plan of action for what to do if victimized.

What can an identity thief do with your personal information?

➤ Go on spending sprees using your credit and debit card account numbers to buy big-ticket items such as computers that they can easily sell.

➤ Open a new credit card account, using your name, date of birth, and SSN. When the thief doesn't pay the bills, the delinquent account is reported on your credit report.

➤ Change the mailing address on your credit card account. The impostor then runs up charges on the account. Because the statement is being sent to the new address, it may take some time before you realize there's a problem.

➤ Take out auto loans in your name.

➤ Establish phone or wireless service in your name.

➤ Counterfeit checks or debit cards, and drain your bank account.

➤ Open a bank account in your name and write bad checks on that account.

➤ File for bankruptcy under your name to avoid paying debts, or to avoid eviction.

➤ Give your name to the police during an arrest. If the thief is released and doesn't show up for the court date, an arrest warrant could be issued in your name.

What action plan should I take to prepare myself in advance in case my identity is stolen?

1. Take a few minutes to capture important information and keep it in a safe place and immediately available:

Make a copy of all the important information in your purse or wallet, including:

➤ All of your credit cards

➤ Your driver's license

➤ Insurance cards

➤ Your ATM card

➤ Your debit card

Next to the credit card information, jot down the telephone number on the back of your card, to call if your card has been lost or stolen.

Write down all of your bank account numbers, including checking accounts, savings accounts, certificates of deposit, lines of credit, and so forth.

Next, visit your bank and write down your branch telephone number, local contact name, and national telephone number to report fraud.

Visit your local police department and write down their telephone number to report fraud.

Write down the three major credit bureaus' names, addresses, and telephone numbers for placing a fraud alert:

➤ **Equifax:** To report fraud, call:
1-800-525-6285, and write: P.O. Box 740241, Atlanta, GA 30374-0241

➤ **Experian:** To report fraud, call:
1-888-EXPERIAN (397-3742), and write: P.O. Box 9532, Allen, TX 75013

➤ **TransUnion:** To report fraud, call:
1-800-680-7289, and write: Fraud Victim Assistance Division, P.O. Box 6790, Fullerton, CA 92834-6790

Write down the telephone number of your state Department of Motor Vehicles to report that your license has been stolen or lost.

Call the Social Security Administration fraud line: 800-269-0271.

You also should be prepared to contact the following major check verification companies. Ask that retailers who use their databases not accept your checks.

TeleCheck: 1-800-710-9898 or 927-0188

Certegy, Inc.: 1-800-437-5120

International Check Services: 1-800-631-9656

Call Shared Check Authorization Network (SCAN) (1-800-262-7771) to find out if the identity thief has been passing bad checks in your name.

2. Be prepared to file a complaint with the Federal Trade Commission (FTC).

   By sharing your identity theft complaint with the FTC, you will provide important information that can help law enforcement track down identity thieves and stop them. The FTC also can refer victim complaints to other appropriate government agencies and companies for further action. The FTC enters the information you provide into its secure database.

   FTC Identity Theft Hotline: 1-877-ID THEFT (438-4338)

3. Get a second photo ID, such as a duplicate driver's license or passport. This is particularly important if you are out of town, because positive ID is required to board airplanes, enter secured buildings, and the like.

Okay, you're prepared now, and if you unfortunately find yourself the victim of identity theft, this is the course of action you should take *immediately*:

➤ File a police report immediately in the jurisdiction where the information was stolen; this proves to credit providers you were diligent, and is a first step toward an investigation (if there ever is one). Make sure to get a copy of your report.

➤ Contact the three major credit bureaus.

➤ Contact your credit card companies.

➤ Call your bank and have them place a freeze on all of your accounts, ATM card, and debit card.

➤ Call the Department of Motor Vehicles.

➤ Contact the major check verification companies.

➤ If necessary, change the locks on your house and car.

➤ Complete an ID theft affidavit and send completed copies to the major credit bureaus, credit card companies, and your bank, but NOT to the FTC or other governmental agencies.

➤ Send a complaint to the FTC at www.consumer.gov/idtheft, or call 1-877-ID-THEFT.

How is someone's identity typically stolen?   Identity thieves may use a variety of low-and high-tech methods to gain access to your personal identifying information. For example:

1. They get information from businesses or institutions by:

   ➤ Stealing records from their employer

   ➤ Bribing an employee who has access to the records

➤ Conning information out of employees

➤ Hacking into the organization's computers

2. They rummage through your trash, the trash of businesses, or dumps, in a practice known as "dumpster diving."

3. They obtain credit reports by abusing their employer's authorized access to credit reports or by posing as a landlord, employer, or someone else who may have a legitimate need for and a legal right to the information.

4. They steal wallets and purses containing identification and credit and bank cards.

5. They steal mail, including bank and credit card statements, preapproved credit offers, new checks, or tax information.

6. They complete a Change of Address form to divert mail to another location.

7. They steal personal information from your home.

8. They scam information from you by posing as a legitimate businessperson or government official.

ID Theft Prevention

What are the best ways for people to protect themselves from identity theft? There are several, and they are all very important:

The Mail   Never use the mailbox outside of your house to mail bills, credit card payments, and the like; drop this mail off at the post office or in an official post office location. People often have a bad habit of putting payments in their home mailbox, and of course putting up the flag to alert the mail carrier that they have mail to be picked up. Unfortunately, this also alerts identity thieves that there may be important personal information in the mailbox, and it is a simple matter of driving through a neighborhood before the mail truck arrives and removing such things as telephone bills, credit card payments, and the like. The thief now of course has the victim's checking account number, credit card number, and *address*.

Never have important information such as credit card bills, bank statements, retirement statements, securities statements, and so forth mailed to your house; get yourself a post office box and have this information mailed to your box.

A variation of the prior example is when a thief waits until *after* the mail carrier *delivers* the mail and drives through a neighborhood opening mailboxes and removing this information. Once again, they have the victim's account numbers.

Unsolicited, Preapproved Credit Cards, Loans, and the Like   Everyone gets this type of information on a regular basis. When you do, don't just put this data in the trash—shred it or rip it up. It is a very easy matter for someone to get this information out of your trash and activate credit cards or loans in your name. (Note: See "'Opting Out' Options," later in this Section.)

Personal Checks   The next time you have checks printed, consider taking the following steps:

➤ Don't imprint your full name; only imprint your *initials* and last name, but on your checking account signature card at the bank, use your full name. If someone intercepts your checks, he will not know your full name or how you sign your checks, but the bank will know, reducing the possibility of passing these checks.

➤ As stated previously, have your bank statements mailed to a post office box, not to your home address, and imprint the post office box address on your checks. You clearly do not want a thief to know where you live. You could also pick up your statements directly at your bank.

➤ Most banks offer customers the ability to check their statements, including checks online. It is a good idea to check your accounts periodically before receiving the actual statement.

➤ Consider getting the type of checks that cannot be scanned. When someone scans this type of check, on the scanned document the words VOID or NOT AN ORIGINAL DOCUMENT appear on the scanned copy, eliminating the possibility of cashing a check more than once.

➤ If you write a lot of checks, consider a bank's Positive Pay service. With this service, one advises the bank (usually electronically) of the check numbers and amounts, and the bank matches this information to checks presented for payment. Any checks that have been altered or presented more than once will not be honored.

➤ Once again, if you write a lot of checks, consider purchasing a check imprinter machine, making altering checks virtually impossible.

➤ When you pay credit card bills by check, only write down the last four numbers of your account number on the FOR line, not the entire number. The credit card company knows the rest of your number, and this way people who come into contact with your check during processing won't have access to your entire account number.

➤ NEVER have your Social Security number or driver's license number imprinted on your check.

➤ Don't have your home telephone number imprinted on your check.

➤ Many merchants now utilize a system (electronic check conversion) whereby checks presented to them at check-out are processed electronically. This is very safe, but remember to get your original check *back*. If you don't get your check back, a disreputable person could both process a payment electronically *and* cash the paper check.

➤ Write checks using a gel pen rather than an ink pen. A knowledgeable person can easily change the payee and amount on a check written in ink.

How?

By placing a piece of tape over the writer's signature to protect it, and dipping the check in a common household liquid. This liquid eradicates the payee and check amount, but the printer's ink on the check is not affected. The thief then simply changes the payee and amounts.

Money Orders and Cashier's Checks   Try to limit the number of checks you write to as few as possible. When checks are necessary, however, consider paying by money order or cashier's check. These are relatively inexpensive, and the security is clearly worth the additional expense.

Debit Memoranda   For routine expenditures such as insurance payments, car payments, mortgage payments, and the like, see if the payment can be made via a direct deduction from your account, called a debit memorandum, or DM. This method is safe and easy, and you'll never have to worry about a late payment. The fewer the checks, the better.

Your Bank Statement and the Uniform Commercial Code (UCC)   Talk to your banker and become aware of the UCC provisions because they may apply to you. Briefly, if your account has been compromised, you have an obligation to advise your bank within a "reasonable" amount of time. Failure to do so may result in your not recovering all of your loss.

Remember, **open your bank statements *immediately*, and review the checks that have cleared the bank.** If you discover a problem, it is your responsibility to advise your bank as soon as possible.

Personal Identification Numbers (PINs)   Often, people have a bad habit of having PIN numbers that are relatively easy to predict. If you do this, a knowledgeable thief can possibly access *all* of your accounts through your bank's website!

Avoid having a PIN that is a combination of the following:

➤ Your initials
➤ Your birth year
➤ Your birthday
➤ Your home address
➤ Your telephone number
➤ Your Social Security number
➤ Your mother's maiden name
➤ Consecutive or repetitive numbers such as 1234, 9999

Use Credit Cards, Debit Cards, and ATM Machines When Possible   Use of these cards is actually very safe when compared to the use of checks, and these companies are very responsible when responding to problems, tracking purchases, putting cards on hold, canceling cards, and so forth.

A few important points to remember when using these cards:

Do

➢ Sign new cards immediately upon receipt.

➢ Save your receipts and compare them to the billing statements.

➢ Open your statement right away and report any suspicious or fraudulent transactions immediately to the credit card company. As in the case of fraudulent checks, the sooner you report problems, the better your chances are to recover a loss.

➢ Have your statement mailed to your post office box rather than your home.

➢ Keep a current record of your account numbers and the telephone number to call to report fraud.

➢ Rip up carbon copies at restaurants, stores, and the like.

➢ Notify card companies of address changes.

➢ Void incorrect charges and keep a record.

➢ Cross out blank spaces above the total.

➢ If you can, pay your credit card bill at the bank, online, or by money order.

➢ Have your photo imprinted on the card when possible.

Don't

➢ Sign blank or untotaled receipts.

➢ Lend your card to anyone.

➢ Write your account number on the outside of remittance envelopes.

➢ Write your full account number in the FOR line of a check. Just use the last four digits.

➢ Give your account number over the telephone unless you are certain the business is reputable.

➢ Carry cards you won't be using.

➢ Write your PIN on your card.

Important Note:

If your card has been used fraudulently, lost, or stolen, you have a responsibility to inform the issuer *immediately*; keep a record of the date, time, and the name of the person you talked to.

If you follow this procedure, by law you are not held responsible for unauthorized charges and your maximum personal liability may be only $50 per card.

Here is your potential liability:

➢ If you report the incident within two business days, your maximum exposure is $50 per card.

➤ If you don't report the loss within two business days, your exposure may be up to $500 per card.

➤ If you fail to report the loss within 60 days of the date of the statement, you could possibly face unlimited loss!

Payroll Checks   If your employer offers direct deposit of payroll checks, it is wise to take advantage of this service, because checks can be lost or stolen, and with direct deposit you don't have to worry about getting your paycheck deposited when you are out sick, on vacation, and so forth.

Computer Issues   Your computer can be a goldmine of personal information to an identity thief. Here's how you can safeguard your computer and the personal information it stores:

➤ **Update your virus protection software regularly.** Computer viruses can have damaging effects, including introducing program code that causes your computer to send out files or other stored information. Look for security repairs and patches you can download from your operating system's website.

➤ **Don't download files from strangers or click on hyperlinks from people you don't know.** Opening a file could expose your system to a computer virus or a program that could hijack your modem.

➤ **Use a firewall,** especially if you have a high-speed or "always on" connection to the Internet. The firewall allows you to limit uninvited access to your computer. Without a firewall, hackers can take over your computer and access sensitive information.

➤ **Use a secure browser**—software that encrypts or scrambles information you send over the Internet—to guard the safety of your online transactions. When you're submitting information, look for the "lock" icon on the status bar. It's a symbol that your information is secure during transmission.

➤ **Obtain automatic upgrades.** We recommend that you purchase a program that automatically upgrades your virus protection on a recurring basis. If you currently do not have an automatic upgrade feature, make sure you update your virus detection program when you hear of a new virus.

➤ **Don't open attachments or diskettes unless you are confident you can trust the source.** Learn how to manually screen diskettes and attachments that antivirus software does not automatically screen for viruses.

➤ **Don't respond to unsolicited emails.** And be careful when clicking on links of unsolicited emails.

➤ **Remember to sign off when through,** and disconnect from the Internet.

➤ **Don't share your password,** and be sure to change it occasionally.

➤ **Be careful to remove information** when selling, trading in, or trashing your computer.

Pretexting   Pretexting is the practice of getting someone's personal information under false pretenses. Pretexters sell your information to people who may use it to get credit in your name, steal your assets, or to investigate or sue you. Pretexting is against the law.

Pretexters use a variety of tactics to get your personal information. For example, a pretexter may call, claim he's from a survey firm, and ask you a few questions. When the pretexter has the information he wants, he uses it to call your financial institution. He pretends to be you or someone with authorized access to your account. He might claim that he's forgotten his checkbook and needs information about his account. In this way, the pretexter may be able to obtain personal information about you, such as your SSN, bank and credit card account numbers, information in your credit report, and the existence and size of your savings and investment portfolios.

Keep in mind that some information about you may be a matter of public record, such as whether you own a home, pay your real estate taxes, or have ever filed for bankruptcy. It is not pretexting for another person to collect this kind of information.

By law, it's illegal for anyone to:

➤ Use false, fictitious or fraudulent statements or documents to get customer information from a financial institution or directly from a customer of a financial institution.

➤ Use forged, counterfeit, lost, or stolen documents to get customer information from a financial institution or directly from a customer of a financial institution.

➤ Ask another person to get someone else's customer information using false, fictitious or fraudulent statements or using false, fictitious or fraudulent documents or forged, counterfeit, lost, or stolen documents.

Buying a Registration Service   For an annual fee, companies will notify the issuers of your credit card and your ATM or debit card accounts if your card is lost or stolen. This service allows you to make only one phone call to report all card losses rather than calling individual issuers. Most services also will request replacement cards on your behalf.

Purchasing a card registration service may be convenient, but it's not required. The FCBA and the EFTA give you the right to contact your card issuers directly in the event of a loss or suspected unauthorized use.

If you decide to buy a registration service, compare offers. Carefully read the contract to determine the company's obligation and your liability. For example, will the company reimburse you if it fails to notify card issuers promptly once you've called in the loss to the service? If not, you could be liable for unauthorized charges or transfers.

Federal Agencies   The following federal agencies are responsible for enforcing federal laws that govern credit card and ATM or debit card transactions. Questions concerning a particular card issuer should be directed to the enforcement agency responsible for that issuer.

Board of Governors of the Federal Reserve System
Regulates state-chartered banks that are members of the Federal Reserve System, bank holding companies, and branches of foreign banks:
Division of Consumer and Community Affairs, Stop 801
20th and C Streets, NW
Washington, DC 20551
202-452-3693
www.federalreserve.gov

Federal Deposit Insurance Corporation
Regulates state-chartered banks that are not members of the Federal Reserve System:
Division of Compliance and Consumer Affairs
550 17th Street, NW
Washington, DC 20429
877-ASK-FDIC (275-3342) toll-free
www.fdic.gov

National Credit Union Administration
Regulates federally chartered credit unions:
Office of Public and Congressional Affairs
1775 Duke Street
Alexandria, VA 22314-3428
703-518-6330
www.ncua.gov

Office of the Comptroller of the Currency
Regulates banks with "National" in the name or "N.A." after the name:
Office of the Ombudsman
Customer Assistance Group
1301 McKinney Street, Suite 3710
Houston, TX 77010
800-613-6743 toll-free
www.occ.treas.gov

Office of Thrift Supervision
Regulates federal savings and loan associations and federal savings banks:
Consumer Programs
1700 G Street, NW
Washington, DC 20551
800-842-6929 toll-free
www.ots.treas.gov

Federal Trade Commission
Regulates other credit card and debit card issuers:
Consumer Response Center
600 Pennsylvania Avenue, NW
Washington, DC 20580
877-FTC-HELP (382-4357) toll-free
www.ftc.gov

The FTC works for the consumer to prevent fraudulent, deceptive, and unfair business practices in the marketplace and to provide information to help consumers spot, stop, and avoid them. To file a complaint or to get free information on consumer issues, go to www.ftc.gov or call toll-free, 1-877-FTC-HELP (1-877-382-4357); TTY: 1-866-653-4261. The FTC enters Internet, telemarketing, identity theft, and other fraud-related complaints into *Consumer Sentinel,* a secure, online database available to hundreds of criminal law enforcement agencies in the U.S. and abroad.

Your Social Security Number   Your Social Security number is the most important personal number you have, so be very careful when giving it out.

It is obviously easy to find out someone's name, address and telephone number, and employment information. It is also relatively easy to get credit history by posing as a merchant and purchasing a credit report. Other critical information important to a thief, such as your mother's maiden name and prior addresses, is simple to obtain, because it is a matter of public record.

When this information is combined with a Social Security number, however, *look out*, because armed with this information an identity thief could:

> Get a driver's license in your name
> Open up loans in your name
> Get credit cards in your name
> Finance a car in your name
> Get wireless telephones in your name
> Get a job in your name
> and on, and on, and on!!

If it appears that someone is using your SSN when applying for a job, get in touch with the Social Security Administration (SSA) to verify the accuracy of your reported earnings and that your name is reported correctly. Call (800) 772-1213 to check your Social Security Statement.

In addition, the SSA may issue you a new SSN at your request if, after trying to resolve the problems brought on by identity theft, you continue to experience problems. Consider this option carefully. A new SSN may not resolve your identity theft problems, and may actually create new problems. For example, a new SSN does not necessarily ensure a new credit record because credit bureaus may combine the credit records from your old SSN with those from your new SSN. Even when the old credit information is not associated with your new SSN, the absence of any credit history under your new SSN may make it more difficult for you to get credit. And finally, there's no guarantee that a new SSN wouldn't also be misused by an identity thief.

If you suspect that your name or SSN is being used by an identity thief to get a driver's license, report it to your Department of Motor Vehicles. Also, if your state uses your SSN as your driver's license number, ask to substitute another number.

To replace your Social Security card, call 1-800-772-1213.

The Social Security Administration Fraud Hotline is 1-800-269-0271.

"Opting Out" Options   Spam, junk mail, and unwanted telemarketers are more than just an annoyance; they are often thinly veiled attempts to commit identity theft by cleverly securing an unsuspecting person's Social Security number, bank account numbers, credit card numbers, and so forth.

While certainly not foolproof, there are several opportunities to "opt out" of receiving these undesired emails and the like.

What can you stop—and what can't you stop?   Federal privacy laws give you the right to stop (opt out of) some sharing of your personal financial information. These laws balance your right to privacy with financial companies' need to share information for normal business purposes. (For more information on these laws, see the appendix on the FCC website.) You have the right to opt out of some information sharing with companies that are:

➤ Part of the same corporate group as your financial company (or affiliates)

➤ Not part of the same corporate group as your financial company (or nonaffiliates)

But you cannot opt out and completely stop the flow of all your personal financial information. The law permits your financial companies to share certain information about you without giving you the right to opt out. Among other things, your financial company can provide to nonaffiliates:

➤ Information about you to firms that help promote and market the company's own products or products offered under a joint agreement between two financial companies

➤ Records of your transactions—such as your loan payments, credit card or debit card purchases, and checking and savings account statements—to firms that provide data processing and mailing services for your company

➤ Information about you in response to a court order

➤ Your payment history on loans and credit cards to credit bureaus

Opting Out of Preapproved Credit Cards and Loans   The credit bureaus offer a toll-free number to call to opt out of having preapproved credit offers sent to you for two years. Call 1-888-5-OPTOUT (567-8688) for more information. When you call, you'll be asked for personal information, including your home telephone number, your name, and your Social Security number. The information you provide is confidential and will be used to process your request to opt out of receiving pre-screened offers of credit.

In addition, you can notify the three major credit bureaus that you do not want personal information about you shared for promotional purposes. Write your own letter or use the sample letter to limit the amount of information the credit bureaus will share about you. Send your letter to the three major credit bureaus:

Equifax, Inc.
Options
P.O. Box 740123
Atlanta, GA 30374-0123

Experian
Consumer Opt-Out
701 Experian Parkway
Allen, TX 75013

TransUnion
Marketing List Opt Out
P.O. Box 97328
Jackson, MS 39288-7328

Opting Out of Telemarketing The federal government has created the National Do Not Call Registry—the free, easy way to reduce the telemarketing calls you get at home. To register, or to get information, visit www.donotcall.gov, or call 1-888-382-1222 from the phone you want to register. You will receive fewer telemarketing calls within three months of registering your number. Your phone number will stay in the registry for five years or until it is disconnected or you take it off the registry. After five years, you will be able to renew your registration.

Opting Out of Junk Mail The Direct Marketing Association's (DMA) Mail Preference Service lets you opt out of receiving direct mail marketing from many national companies for five years. When you register with this service, your name will be put on a "delete" file and made available to direct mail marketers. However, your registration will not stop mailings from organizations that are not registered with the DMS's Mail Preference Service. To register with DMA, send your letter to:

Direct Marketing Association
Mail Preference Service
P.O. Box 643
Carmel, NY 10512

Or register online at www.the-dma.org/consumers/offmailinglist.html.

Opting Out of Unsolicited Email   The DMA also has an Email Preference Service to help you reduce unsolicited commercial emails. To opt out of receiving unsolicited commercial email, use DMA's online form at www.dmaconsumers.org/offemaillist.html. Your online request will be effective for one year.

For More Information

To learn more about privacy issues and how they affect your life and the decisions you may make in the marketplace, visit www.ftc.gov/privacy.

Credit Bureaus: Sample Opt-Out Letter

Be sure to send your letter to ALL three credit bureaus.

Date

To whom it may concern:

I request to have my name removed from your marketing lists. Here is the information you have asked me to include in my request:

FIRST, MIDDLE & LAST NAME
(List all name variations, including Jr., Sr., etc.)

_____

CURRENT MAILING ADDRESS

_____

_____

PREVIOUS MAILING ADDRESS
(Fill in your previous mailing address if you have moved in the last 6 months.)

_____

_____

SOCIAL SECURITY NUMBER

_____

DATE OF BIRTH

_____

Thank you for your prompt handling of my request.

_____

Signature

Electronic Banking For many consumers, electronic banking means 24-hour access to cash through an automated teller machine (ATM) or direct deposit of paychecks into checking or savings accounts. But electronic banking now involves many different types of transactions.

Electronic banking, also known as electronic fund transfer (EFT), uses computer and electronic technology as a substitute for checks and other paper transactions. EFTs are initiated through devices such as cards or codes that let you, or those you authorize, access your account. Many financial institutions use ATM or debit cards and personal identification numbers for this purpose. Some use other forms of debit cards such as those that require, at the most, your signature or a scan. The federal Electronic Fund Transfer Act (EFT Act) covers some electronic consumer transactions.

Electronic Fund Transfers EFT offers several services that consumers may find practical:

➤ Automated teller machines, or 24-hour tellers, are electronic terminals that let you bank almost any time. To withdraw cash, make deposits, or transfer funds between accounts, you generally insert an ATM card and enter your PIN. Some financial institutions and ATM owners charge a fee, particularly to consumers who don't have accounts with them or on transactions at remote locations. Generally, ATMs must tell you they charge a fee and its amount, on or at the terminal screen, before you complete the transaction. Check the rules of your institution and ATMs you use to find out when or whether a fee is charged.

➤ Direct deposit lets you authorize specific deposits, such as paychecks and Social Security checks, to your account on a regular basis. You also may preauthorize direct withdrawals so that recurring bills, such as insurance premiums, mortgages, and utility bills, are paid automatically.

➤ Pay-by-phone systems let you call your financial institution with instructions to pay certain bills or to transfer funds between accounts. You must have an agreement with the institution to make such transfers.

➤ Personal computer banking lets you handle many banking transactions via your personal computer. For instance, you may use your computer to view your account balance, request transfers between accounts, and pay bills electronically.

➤ Point-of-sale transfers let you pay for purchases with a debit card, which also may be your ATM card. The process is similar to using a credit card, with some important exceptions. The process is fast and easy, but a debit card purchase transfers money—fairly quickly—from your bank account to the store's account. So it's important that you have funds in your account to cover your purchase. This means you need to keep accurate records of the dates and amounts of your debit card purchases and ATM withdrawals, in addition to any checks you write. Your liability for unauthorized use, and your rights for error resolution, may differ with a debit card. Nonauthorized use of a check or credit card is relatively easy to document and the consumer is usually made whole by the bank or credit card company as long as the complaint is filed timely. However, debit card transactions fall under a different law called the Electronic Funds Transfer Act, and the liability facing the defrauded debit cardholder depends upon the speed with which the complaint is filed. Briefly, if the complaint is filed within two days, the consumer's liability is $50, but the liability jumps to $500 if the complaint is between three and sixty days. If the complaint isn't filed within sixty days, the liability for unauthorized used after sixty days shifts to the consumer.

➤ Electronic check conversion converts a paper check into an electronic payment at the point of sale or elsewhere, such as when a company receives your check in the mail. In a store, when you give your check to a store cashier, the check is processed through an electronic system that captures your banking information and the amount of the check. Once the check is processed, you're asked to sign a receipt authorizing the merchant to present the check to your bank electronically and deposit the funds into the merchant's account. You get a receipt of the electronic transaction for your records. When your check has been processed and returned to you by the merchant, it should be voided or marked by the merchant so that it can't be used again. In the mail-in situation, you should still receive advance notice from a company that expects to process your check electronically.

Be especially careful in telephone transactions, which also could involve e-checks. A legitimate merchant should explain the process and answer any questions you may have. The merchant also should ask for your permission to debit your account for the item you're purchasing or paying on. However, because telephone e-check transactions don't occur face-to-face, you should be cautious to whom you reveal your bank or checking account information. Don't give this information to sellers with whom you have no prior experience or with whom you have not initiated the call, or to sellers who seem reluctant to discuss the process with you.

Not all electronic fund transfers are covered by the EFT Act. For example, some financial institutions and merchants issue cards with cash value stored electronically on the card itself. Examples include prepaid telephone cards, mass transit passes, and some gift cards. These stored-value cards, as well as transactions using them, may not be covered by the EFT Act. This means you may not be covered for the loss or misuse of the card. Ask your financial institution or merchant about any protections offered for these cards.

Limited Stop-Payment Privileges   When you use an electronic fund transfer, the EFT Act does not give you the right to stop payment. If your purchase is defective or your order is not delivered, it's as if you paid cash. That is, it's up to you to resolve the problem with the seller and get your money back.

There is one situation, however, when you can stop payment. If you've arranged for regular payments out of your account to third parties, such as insurance companies, you can stop payment if you notify your institution at least three business days before the scheduled transfer. The notice may be oral or written, but the institution may require a written follow-up within 14 days of the oral notice. If you fail to provide the written follow-up, the institution's responsibility to stop payment ends.

Although federal law provides only limited rights to stop payment, individual financial institutions may offer more rights, or state laws may require them. If this feature is important to you, you may want to shop around to be sure you're getting the best stop-payment terms available.

Where to File Complaints   If you think a financial institution or company has failed to fulfill its responsibilities to you under the EFT Act, speak up. In addition, you may wish to complain to the federal agency listed below that has enforcement jurisdiction over that company.

State Member Banks of the Federal Reserve System
Consumer and Community Affairs
Board of Governors of the Federal Reserve System
20th & C Streets, NW, Mail Stop 801
Washington, DC 20551
www.federalreserve.gov

National Banks
Office of the Comptroller of the Currency
Compliance Management
Mail Stop 7-5
Washington, DC 20219
www.occ.treas.gov

Federal Credit Unions
National Credit Union Administration
1775 Duke Street
Alexandria, VA 22314
www.ncua.gov

Non-Member Federally Insured Banks
Office of Consumer Programs
Federal Deposit Insurance Corporation
550 17th Street, NW
Washington, DC 20419
www.fdic.gov

Federally Insured Savings and Loans, and Federally Chartered State Banks
Consumer Affairs Program
Office of Thrift Supervision
1700 G Street, NW
Washington, DC 20551
www.ots.treas.gov

How can I tell if I'm a victim of identity theft?   Monitor the balances of your financial accounts. Look for unexplained charges or withdrawals. Other indications of identity theft can be:

➤ Failing to receive bills or other mail, signaling an address change by the identity thief
➤ Receiving credit cards for which you did not apply
➤ Denial of credit for no apparent reason
➤ Receiving calls from debt collectors or companies about merchandise or services you didn't buy

Are there any other steps I can take?   Get a copy of your credit report.

If an identity thief is opening new credit accounts in your name, these accounts are likely to show up on your credit report. You can find out by ordering a copy of your credit report from any of three major credit bureaus. If you find inaccurate information, check your reports from the other two credit bureaus. Of course, some inaccuracies on your credit reports may be caused by computer, clerical, or other errors and may not be a result of identity theft. Note: If your personal information has been lost or stolen, you may want to check all of your reports more frequently for the first year. Federal law allows credit bureaus to charge you up to $9.00 for a copy of your credit report. Some states may allow a free report or reduced rates.

How can I get copies of my credit reports?   Contact each of the three major credit bureaus:

Equifax: www.equifax.com
To order your report, call: 800-685-1111 or write:
P.O. Box 740241, Atlanta, GA 30374-0241

To report fraud, call: 800-525-6285 and write:
P.O. Box 740241, Atlanta, GA 30374-0241
If you are hearing impaired, call 1-800-25-0056 and ask the operator to call the Auto Disclosure Line at 1-800-685-1111 to request a copy of your report.

Experian: www.experian.com
To order your report, call: 888-EXPERIAN (397-3742) or write:
P.O. Box 2002, Allen, TX 75013

To report fraud, call: 888-EXPERIAN (397-3742) and write:
PO. Box 9530, Allen, TX 75013
TDD: 1-800-972-0322

Trans Union: www.transunion.com
To order your report, call: 800-888-4213 or write:
P.O. Box 1000, Chester, PA 19022

To report fraud, call: 800-680-7289 and write:
Fraud Victim Assistance Division, P.O. Box 6790, Fullerton, CA 92634
TDD: 1-877-553-7803

How much does a credit report cost?   Each credit bureau may charge you up to $9.00 for a copy of your report. However, you are entitled to one free report a year if you can show that: Your report is inaccurate because of fraud; you're on welfare; or you're unemployed and plan to look for a job within 60 days. There also is no charge if a company has taken adverse action against you, such as denying your application for credit, insurance, or employment, and you request your report within 60 days of receiving the notice of the adverse action.

Certain states also have passed legislation that entitles you to a free report or a report at a reduced rate.

How do I correct inaccurate information on my credit reports?   The Fair Credit Reporting Act (FCRA) establishes procedures for correcting mistakes on your credit record and requires that your record be made available only for certain legitimate business needs.

Under the FCRA, both the credit bureau and the organization that provided the information to the credit bureau (the "information provider"), such as a bank or credit card company, are responsible for correcting inaccurate or incomplete information in your report. To protect your rights under the law, contact both the credit bureau and the information provider.

First, call the credit bureau and follow up in writing. Tell them what information you believe is inaccurate. Include copies (NOT originals) of documents that support your position. In addition to providing your complete name and address, your letter should clearly identify each item in your report that you dispute, give the facts and explain why you dispute the information, and request deletion or correction. You may want to enclose a copy of your report with circles around the items in question. Send your letter by certified mail, and request a return receipt so you can document what the credit bureau received and when. Keep copies of your letter and enclosures.

Credit bureaus must investigate the items in question—within 30 or 45 days (depending on whether you provide additional information)—unless they consider your dispute frivolous. They also must forward all relevant data you provide about the dispute to the information provider. After the information provider receives notice of a dispute from the credit bureau, it must investigate, review all relevant information provided by the credit bureau, and report the results to the credit bureau. If the information provider finds the disputed information to be inaccurate, it must notify any nationwide credit bureau that it reports to, so that the credit bureaus can correct this information in your file. Note that:

➢ Disputed information that cannot be verified must be deleted from your file.

➢ If your report contains erroneous information, the credit bureau must correct it.

➢ If an item is incomplete, the credit bureau must complete it. For example, if your file shows that you have been late making payments, but fails to show that you are no longer delinquent, the credit bureau must show that you're current.

➢ If your file shows an account that belongs to someone else, the credit bureau must delete it.

When the investigation is complete, the credit bureau must give you the written results and a free copy of your report if the dispute results in a change. If an item is changed or removed, the credit bureau cannot put the disputed information back in your file unless the information provider verifies its accuracy and completeness, and the credit bureau gives you a written notice that includes the name, address, and phone number of the information provider.

If you request, the credit bureau must send notices of corrections to anyone who received your report.

What should I do about unauthorized charges on my credit cards?   The Fair Credit Billing Act (FCBA) establishes procedures for resolving billing errors on your credit card accounts, including fraudulent charges on your accounts, and limits your liability for unauthorized credit card charges to $50 per card.

To take advantage of the law's consumer protections, you must:

➢ Write to the creditor at the address given for billing inquiries, not the address for sending your payments. Include your name, address, account number, and a description of the billing error, including the amount and date of the error.

➢ Send your letter so that it reaches the creditor within 60 days after the first bill containing the error was mailed to you. If the address on your account was changed by an identity thief and you never received the bill, your dispute letter still must reach the creditor within 60 days of when the creditor would have mailed the bill. This is why it's so important to keep track of your billing statements and immediately follow up when your bills don't arrive on time.

➢ Send your letter by certified mail, and request a return receipt. This will be your proof of the date the creditor received the letter. Include copies (NOT originals) of sales slips or other documents that support your position. Keep a copy of your dispute letter.

The creditor must acknowledge your complaint in writing within 30 days after receiving it, unless the problem has been resolved. The creditor must resolve the dispute within two billing cycles (but not more than 90 days) after receiving your letter.

What do I do if someone is using my checks? If your checks have been stolen or misused, close the account and ask your bank to notify the check verification service with which it does business. Although no federal law limits your losses if someone steals your checks and forges your signature, state laws may protect you. Most states hold the bank responsible for losses from a forged check. At the same time, most states require you to take reasonable care of your account. For example, you may be held responsible for the forgery if you fail to notify the bank in a timely manner that a check was lost or stolen. Contact your state banking or consumer protection agency for more information.

You can contact major check verification companies directly for the following services:

➤ To request that they notify retailers who use their databases not to accept your checks, call:

TeleCheck:
1-800-710-9898 or 927-0188

Certegy, Inc. (previously Equifax Check Systems):
1-800-437-5120

➤ To find out if an identity thief has been passing bad checks in your name, call:

SCAN: 1-800-262-7771

How do I get back money that was stolen from my debit card account or through other electronic fund transfers? The Electronic Fund Transfer Act provides consumer protections for transactions involving an ATM or debit card or other electronic means of debiting or crediting an account. It also limits your liability for unauthorized electronic fund transfers.

It's important to report lost or stolen ATM and debit cards immediately because the amount you can be held responsible for depends on **how quickly** you report the loss.

➤ If you report your ATM card lost or stolen within two business days of discovering the loss or theft, your losses are limited to $50.

➤ If you report your ATM card lost or stolen after two business days, but within 60 days after receiving a statement showing an unauthorized electronic fund transfer, you can be liable for up to $500 of what a thief withdraws.

➤ If you wait more than 60 days, you could lose **all** the money that was taken from your account after the end of the 60 days and before you reported your card missing.

The best way to protect yourself in the event of an error or fraudulent transaction is to call the financial institution and follow up in writing—by certified letter, return receipt requested—so you can prove when the institution received your letter. Keep a copy of the letter you send for your records.

After receiving notification about an error on your statement, the institution generally has ten business days to investigate. The financial institution must tell you the results of its investigation within three business days after completing it and must correct an error within one business day after determining that the error has occurred. If the institution needs more time, it may take up to 45 days to complete the investigation—but only if the money in dispute is returned to your account and you are notified promptly of the credit. At the end of the investigation, if no error has been found, the institution may take the money back if it sends you a written explanation.

Note: VISA and MasterCard have voluntarily agreed to limit consumers' liability for unauthorized use of their debit cards in most instances to $50 per card, no matter how much time has elapsed since the discovery of the loss or theft of the card.

What do I do if my bank won't correct the fraud?   If you're having trouble getting your financial institution to help you resolve your banking-related identity theft problems, including problems with bank-issued credit cards, contact the agency with the appropriate jurisdiction. If you're not sure which agency has jurisdiction over your institution, call your bank or contact your state attorney general.

Fair Credit Reporting and Collection Agencies   If you've ever applied for a charge account, a personal loan, insurance, or a job, there's a file about you. This file contains information on where you work and live, how you pay your bills, and whether you've been sued or arrested, or have field for bankruptcy.

Companies that gather and sell this information are called consumer reporting agencies (CRAs). The most common type of CRA is the credit bureau. The information CRAs sell about you to creditors, employers, insurers, and other businesses is called a consumer report.

The Fair Credit Reporting Act (FCRA), enforced by the Federal Trade Commission, is designed to promote accuracy and ensure the privacy of the information used in consumer reports. Recent amendments to the Act expand your rights and place additional requirements on CRAs. Businesses that supply information about you to CRAs and those that use consumer reports also have new responsibilities under the law.

Commonly Asked Questions and Answers Concerning Consumer Reports and CRAs:

Q. How do I find the CRA that has my report? A. Contact the CRAs listed in the Yellow Pages under "Credit" or "Credit Rating and Reporting." Because more than one CRA may have a file on you, call each until you locate all the agencies maintaining your file. The three major national credit bureaus are:

Equifax
800-685-1111
www.equifax.com

Experian
888-EXPERIAN (888-397-3742)
www.experian.com

TransUnion
800-916-8800
www.transunion.com

In addition, anyone who takes action against you in response to a report supplied by a CRA—such as denying your application for credit, insurance, or employment—must give you the name, address, and telephone number of the CRA that provided the report.

Q. Do I have a right to know what's in my report? A. Yes, if you ask for it. The CRA must tell you everything in your report, including medical information, and in most cases, the sources of the information. The CRA also must give you a list of everyone who has requested your report within the past year—two years for employment-related requests.

Q. Is there a charge for my report? A. Sometimes. There's no charge if a company takes adverse action against you, such as denying your application for credit, insurance, or employment, and you request your report within 60 days of receiving the notice of the action. The notice will give you the name, address, and phone number of the CRA. In addition, you're entitled to one free report a year if (1) you're unemployed and plan to look for a job within 60 days, (2) you're on welfare, or (3) your report is inaccurate because of fraud. Otherwise, a CRA may charge you up to $9.00 for a copy of your report.

Q. What can I do about inaccurate or incomplete information? A. Under the new law, both the CRA and the information provider have responsibilities for correcting inaccurate or incomplete information in your report. To protect all your rights under this law, contact both the CRA and the information provider.

First, tell the CRA in writing what information you believe is inaccurate. CRAs must reinvestigate the items in questions—usually within 30 days—unless they consider your dispute frivolous. They also must forward all relevant data you provide about the dispute to the information provider. After the information provider receives notice of a dispute from the CRA, it must investigate, review all relevant information provided by the CRA, and report the results to the CRA. If the information provider finds the disputed information to be inaccurate, it must notify all nationwide CRAs so that they can correct this information in your file.

When the reinvestigation is complete, the CRA must give you the written results and a free copy of your report if the dispute results in a change. If an item is changed or removed, the CRA cannot put the disputed information back in your file unless the information provider verifies its accuracy and completeness, and the CRA gives you a written notice that includes the name, address, and phone number of the provider.

Second, tell the creditor or other information provider in writing that you dispute an item. Many providers specify an address for disputes. If the provider then reports the item to any CRA, it must include a notice of your dispute. In addition, if you are correct—that is, if the information is inaccurate—the information provider may not use it again.

Q. What can I do if the CRA or information provider won't correct the information I dispute?   A. A reinvestigation may not resolve your dispute with the CRA. If that's the case, ask the CRA to include your statement of the dispute in your file and in future reports. At your request, the CRA also will provide your statement to anyone who received a copy of the old report in the recent past. There usually is a fee for this service.

If you tell the information provider that you dispute an item, a notice of your dispute must be included anytime the information provider reports the item to a CRA.

Q. Can my employer get my report?   A. Only if you say it's okay. A CRA may not supply information about you to your employer, or to a prospective employer, without your consent.

Q. Can creditors, employers, or insurers get a report that contains medical information about me?   A. Not without your approval.

Q. What should I know about investigative consumer reports?   A. Investigative consumer reports are detailed reports that involve interviews with your neighbors or acquaintances about your lifestyle, character, and reputation. They may be used in connection with insurance and employment applications. You'll be notified in writing when a company orders such a report. The notice will explain your right to request certain information about the report from the company you applied to. If your application is rejected, you may get additional information from the CRA. However, the CRA does not have to reveal the sources of the information.

Q. How long can a CRA report negative information?   A. Seven years. There are certain exceptions:

➤ Information about criminal convictions may be reported without any time limitation.

➤ Bankruptcy information may be reported for 10 years.

➤ Information reported in response to an application for a job with a salary of more than $75,000 has no time limit.

➤ Information reported because of an application for more than $150,000 worth of credit or life insurance has no time limit.

➤ Information about a lawsuit or an unpaid judgment against you can be reported for seven years or until the statute of limitations runs out, whichever is longer.

Q. Can anyone get a copy of my report?   A. No. Only people with a legitimate business need, as recognized by the FCRA. For example, a company is allowed to get your report if you apply for credit, insurance, or employment, or to rent an apartment.

Q. How can I stop a CRA from including me on lists for unsolicited credit and insurance offers?   A. Creditors and insurers may use CRA file information as a basis for sending you unsolicited offers. These offers must include a toll-free number for you to call if you want to remove your name and address from lists for two years; completing a form that the CRA provides for this purpose will keep your name off the lists permanently.

Q. Do I have the right to sue for damages?   A. You may sue a CRA, a user, or—in some cases—a provider of CRA data, in state or federal court for most violations of the FCRA. If you win, the defendant will have to pay damages and reimburse you for attorney fees to the extent ordered by the court.

Q. Are there other laws I should know about?   A. Yes. If your credit application has been denied, the Equal Credit Opportunity Act requires creditors to specify why—if you ask. For example, the creditor must tell you whether you were denied because you have "no credit file" with a CRA or because the CRA says you have "delinquent obligations." The ECOA also requires creditors to consider additional information you might supply about your credit history. You may want to find out why the creditor denied your application before you contact the CRA.

Q. Where should I report violations of the law?   A. Although the FTC can't act as your lawyer in private disputes, information about your experiences and concerns is vital to the enforcement of the Fair Credit Reporting Act. Send your questions or complaints to: Consumer Response Center—FCRA, Federal Trade Commission, Washington, DC 20580.

Fair Debt Collection

If you use credit cards, owe money on a personal loan, or are paying on a home mortgage, you are a debtor. If you fall behind in repaying your creditors, or an error is made on your accounts, you may be contacted by a debt collector.

You should know that, in either situation, the Fair Debt Collection Practices Act requires that debt collectors treat you fairly and prohibits certain methods of debt collection. Of course, the law does not erase any legitimate debt you owe.

What debts are covered?   Personal, family, and household debts are covered under the Act. This includes money owed for the purchase of an automobile, for medical care, or for charge accounts.

Who is a debt collector?   A debt collector is any person who regularly collects debts owed to others. This includes attorneys who collect debts on a regular basis.

How may a debt collector contact you?   A collector may contact you in person, by mail, telephone, telegram, or fax. However, a debt collector may not contact you at inconvenient times or places, such as before 8:00 a.m. or after 9:00 p.m., unless you agree. A debt collector also may not contact you at work if the collector knows that your employer disapproves of such contacts.

Can you stop a debt collector from contacting you?   You can stop a debt collector from contacting you by writing a letter to the collector telling him to stop. Once the collector receives your letter, he may not contact you again except to say there will be no further contact or to notify you that the debt collector or the creditor intends to take some specific action. Please note, however, that sending such a letter to a collector does not make the debt go away if you actually owe it. You could still be sued by the debt collector or your original creditor.

May a debt collector contact anyone else about your debt?   If you have an attorney, the debt collector must contact the attorney, rather than you. If you do not have an attorney, a collector may contact other people, but only to find out where you live, what your phone number is, and where you work. Collectors usually are prohibited from contacting such third parties more than once. In most cases, the collector may not tell anyone other than you and your attorney that you owe money.

What must the debt collector tell you about the debt?   Within five days after you are first contacted, the collector must send you a written notice telling you the amount of money you owe, the name of the creditor to whom you owe the money, and what action to take if you believe you do not owe the money.

May a debt collector continue to contact you if you believe you do not owe money?   A collector may not contact you if, within 30 days after you receive the written notice, you send the collection agency a letter stating you do not owe the money.

However, a collector can renew collection activities if you are sent proof of the debt, such as a copy of a bill for the amount owed.

What types of debt collection practices are prohibited?

Harassment: Debt collectors may not harass, oppress, or abuse you or any third parties they contact. For example, debt collectors may not:

➤ Use threats of violence or harm

➤ Publish a list of consumers who refuse to pay their debts (except to a credit bureau)

➤ Use obscene or profane language

➤ Repeatedly use the telephone to annoy someone

False statements: Debt collectors may not use any false or misleading statements when collecting a debt. For example, debt collectors may not:

➤ Falsely imply that they are attorneys or government representatives

➤ Falsely imply that you have committed a crime

➤ Falsely represent that they operate or work for a credit bureau

➤ Misrepresent the amount of your debt

➤ Indicate that papers being sent to you are legal forms when they are not

➤ Indicate that papers being sent to you are not legal forms when they are

Debt collectors also may not state that:

➤ You will be arrested if you do not pay your debt

➤ They will seize, garnish, attach, or sell your property or wages, unless the collection agency or creditor intends to do so, and it is legal to do so

➤ Actions, such as a lawsuit, will be taken against you, when such action legally may not be taken, or when they do not intend to take such action

Debt collectors may not:

➤ Give false credit information about you to anyone, including a credit bureau

➤ Send you anything that looks like an official document from a court or government agency when it is not

➤ Use a false name

Unfair practices: Debt collectors may not engage in unfair practices when they try to collect a debt. For example, collectors may not:

➤ Collect any amount greater than your debt, unless your state law permits such a charge

➤ Deposit a postdated check prematurely

➤ Use deception to make you accept collect calls or pay for telegrams

➤ Take or threaten to take your property, unless this can be done legally

➤ Contact you by postcard

What control do you have over payment of debts?   If you owe more than one debt, any payment you make must be applied to the debt you indicate. A debt collector may not apply a payment to any debt you believe you do not owe.

What can you do if you believe a debt collector has violated the law?   You have the right to sue a collector in a state or federal court within one year from the date the law was violated. If you win, you may recover money for the damages you suffered plus an additional amount up to $1,000. Court costs and attorney's fees also can be recovered. A group of people also may sue a debt collector and recover money for damages up to $500,000, or one percent of the collector's net worth, whichever is less.

Where can you report a debt collector for an alleged violation?   Report any problems you have with a debt collector to your state attorney general's office and the Federal Trade Commission. Many states have their own debt collection laws, and your attorney general's office can help you determine your rights.

Collection Agencies

If you find yourself the victim of identity theft, there is a possibility that scammed merchants may employ a collection agency to help collect debts on sales they thought were made legitimately. As an innocent identity theft victim, you may be contacted by a collection agency.

How do I stop debt collectors from contacting me?   The Fair Debt Collection Practices Act prohibits debt collectors from using unfair or deceptive practices to collect overdue bills that a creditor has forwarded for collection.

You can stop a debt collector from contacting you by writing a letter to the collection agency telling them to stop. Once the debt collector receives your letter, the company may not contact you again—with two exceptions: They can tell you there will be no further contact, and they can tell you that the debt collector or the creditor intends to take some specific action.

A collector also may not contact you if, within 30 days after you receive the written notice, you send the collection agency a letter stating that you do not owe the money. In this case, a collector can renew collection activities if you are sent proof of the debt. So, along with your letter stating that you don't owe the money, include copies of documents that support your position. Including a copy (NOT an original) of the police report you filed may be particularly useful.

If you don't have documentation to support your position, be as specific as possible about why the debt collector is mistaken. The debt collector is responsible for sending you proof that you're wrong. For example, if the debt in dispute originates from a credit card you never applied for, ask for the actual application containing the applicant's signature. You can then prove that it's not your signature on the application. However, in many cases, the debt collector will not send you any proof, but will instead return the debt to the creditor.

Remember, you can stop the debt collectors from contacting you, but that won't necessarily get rid of the debt itself. It's important to contact the creditors individually to dispute the debt; otherwise, the creditor may send it to a different debt collector, report it on your credit report, or institute a lawsuit.

For more information, consult "Fair Debt Collection," above.

Fair Credit Billing

Have you ever been billed for merchandise you returned or never received? Has your credit card company ever charged you twice for the same item or failed to credit a payment to your account? While frustrating, these errors can be corrected. It takes a little patience and knowledge of the dispute settlement procedures provided by the Fair Credit Billing Act (FCBA).

The law applies to "open end" credit accounts (such as credit cards) and revolving charge accounts (such as department store accounts). It does not cover installment contracts—loans or extensions of credit you repay on a fixed schedule. Consumers often buy cars, furniture, and major appliances on an installment basis, and repay personal loans in installments as well.

What types of disputes are covered?   The FCBA settlement procedures apply only to disputes about "billing errors." For example:

➤ Unauthorized charges; federal law limits your responsibility for unauthorized charges to $50

➤ Charges that list the wrong date or amount

➤ Charges for goods and services that you didn't accept or that weren't delivered as agreed

➤ Math errors

➤ Failure to post payments and other credits, such as returns

➤ Failure to send bills to your current address—provided the creditor receives your change of address, in writing, at least 20 days before the billing period ends

➤ Charges for which you ask for an explanation or written proof of purchase along with a claimed error or request for clarification

To take advantage of the law's consumer protections, you must:

➤ Write to the creditor at the address given for "billing inquiries," not the address for sending your payments, and include your name, address, account number, and a description of the billing error

➤ Send your letter so that it reaches the creditor within 60 days after the first bill containing the error was mailed to you

Send your letter by certified mail, return receipt requested, so you have proof of what the creditor received. Include copies (not originals) of sales slips or other documents that support your position. Keep a copy of your dispute letter.

The creditor must acknowledge your complaint in writing within 30 days after receiving it, unless the problem has been resolved. The creditor must resolve the dispute within two billing cycles (but not more than 90 days) after receiving your letter. A sample letter follows.

Date
Your Name
Your Address
Your City, State, Zip Code
Your Account Number

Name of Creditor
Billing Inquiries
Address
City, State, Zip Code

Dear Sir or Madam:

I am writing to dispute a billing error in the amount of $_____ on my account. The amount is inaccurate because (describe the problem). I am requesting that the error be corrected, that any finance and other charges related to the disputed amount be credited as well, and that I receive an accurate statement.

Enclosed are copies of (use this sentence to describe any enclosed information, such as sales slips, payments records) supporting my position. Please investigate this matter and correct the billing error as soon as possible.

Sincerely,
Your name
Enclosures: (list what you are enclosing)

What happens while my bill is in dispute?   You may withhold payment on the disputed amount (and related charges) during the investigation. You must pay any part of the bill not in question, including finance charges on the undisputed amount.

The creditor may not take any legal or other action to collect the disputed amount and related charges (including finance charges) during the investigation. Although your account cannot be closed or restricted, the disputed amount may be applied against your credit limit.

Will my credit rating be affected?   The creditor may not threaten your credit rating or report you as delinquent while your bill is in dispute. However, the creditor may report that you are challenging your bill. In addition, the Equal Credit Opportunity Act prohibits creditors from discriminating against credit applicants who exercise their rights, in good faith, under the FCBA. Simply put, you cannot be denied credit simply because you've disputed a bill.

What if the bill is incorrect?   If your bill contains an error, the creditor must explain to you—in writing—the corrections that will be made to your account. In addition to crediting your account, the creditor must remove all finance charges, late fees, or other charges related to the error.

If the creditor determines that you owe a portion of the disputed amount, you must get a written explanation. You may request copies of documents proving you owe the money.

What if the bill is correct?   If the creditor's investigation determines the bill is correct, you must be told promptly and in writing how much you owe and why. You may ask for copies of relevant documents. At this point, you'll owe the disputed amount, plus any finance charges that accumulated while the amount was in dispute. You also may have to pay the minimum amount you missed paying because of the dispute.

If you disagree with the results of the investigation, you may write to the creditor, but you must act within 10 days after receiving the explanation, and you may indicate that you refuse to pay the disputed amount. At this point, the creditor may begin collection procedures. However, if the creditor reports you to a credit bureau as delinquent, the report also must state that you don't think you owe the money. The creditor must tell you who gets these reports.

What if the creditor fails to follow the procedure?   Any creditor who fails to follow the settlement procedure may not collect the amount in dispute, or any related finance charges, up to $50, even if the bill turns out to be correct. For example, if a creditor acknowledges your complaint in 45 days—15 days too late—or takes more than two billing cycles to resolve a dispute, the penalty applies. The penalty also applies if a creditor threatens to report—or improperly reports—your failure to pay to anyone during the dispute period.

An Important Caveat   Disputes about the quality of goods and services are not "billing errors," so the dispute procedure does not apply. However, if you buy unsatisfactory goods or services with a credit or charge card, you can take the same legal actions against the card issuer as you can take under state law against the seller.

To take advantage of this protection regarding the quality of goods or services, you must:

➤ Have made the purchase (it must be for more than $50) in your home state or within 100 miles of your current billing address

➤ Make a good faith effort to resolve the dispute with the seller first

The dollar and distance limitations don't apply if the seller also is the card issuer, or if a special business relationship exists between the seller and the card issuer.

Other Billing Rights   Businesses that offer "open end" credit also must:

➤ Give you a written notice when you open a new account—and at certain other times—that describes your right to dispute billing errors.

➤ Provide a statement for each billing period in which you owe—or they owe you—more than one dollar.

➤ Send your bill at least 14 days before the payment is due—if you have a period within which to pay the bill without incurring additional charges.

➤ Credit all payments to your account on the date they're received, unless no extra charges would result if they failed to do so. Creditors are permitted to set some reasonable rules for making payments—say, setting a reasonable deadline for payment to be received to be credited on the same date.

➤ Promptly credit or refund overpayments and other amounts owed to your account. This applies to instances where your account is owed more than one dollar. Your account must be credited promptly with the amount owed. If you prefer a refund, it must be sent within seven business days after the creditor receives your written request. The creditor must also make a good faith effort to refund a credit balance that has remained on your account for more than six months.

Suing the Creditor   You can sue a creditor who violates the FCBA. If you win, you may be awarded damages, plus twice the amount of any finance charge—as long as it's between $100 and $1,000. The court also may order the creditor to pay your attorney's fees and costs.

If possible, hire a lawyer who is willing to accept the amount awarded to you by the court for attorney's fees as the entire fee for representing you. Some lawyers may not take your case unless you agree to pay their fee—win or lose—or add to the court-awarded amount if they think it's too low.

Reporting FCBA Violations The Federal Trade Commission (FTC) enforces the FCBA for most creditors except banks. The FTC works for the consumer to prevent fraudulent, deceptive, and unfair business practices in the marketplace and to provide information to help consumers spot, stop, and avoid them. To file a complaint or to get free information on consumer issues, call toll-free, 1-877-FTC-HELP (1-877-382-4357), or use the complaint form at www.ftc.gov. The FTC enters Internet, telemarketing, identity theft, and other fraud-related complaints into Consumer Sentinel, a secure, online database available to hundreds of civil and criminal law enforcement agencies in the U.S. and abroad.

Bankruptcy

What do I do if someone has filed for bankruptcy in my name? If you believe someone has filed for bankruptcy in your name, write to the U.S. Trustee (UST) in the region where the bankruptcy was filed. A list of the U.S. Trustee Program's regional offices is available on the UST website, or check the Blue Pages of your phone book under U.S. Government Bankruptcy Administration.

Your letter should describe the situation and provide proof of your identity. The U.S. Trustee, if appropriate, will make a criminal referral to law enforcement authorities if you provide appropriate documentation to substantiate your claim. You also may want to file a complaint with the U.S. Attorney and/or the FBI in the city where the bankruptcy was filed. The U.S. Trustee does not provide legal representation, legal advice, or referrals to lawyers. That means you may need to hire an attorney to help convince the bankruptcy court that the filing is fraudulent. The U.S. Trustee does not provide consumers with copies of court documents. Those documents are available from the bankruptcy clerk's office for a fee.

For more information, see U.S. Trustee: www.usdoj.gov/ust.

Criminal Records

What do I do about criminal records incurred in my name? Although procedures to correct your record within criminal justice databases vary from state to state, and even from county to county, the following information can be used as a general guide.

If criminal violations are wrongfully attributed to your name, contact the arresting or citing law enforcement agency—that is, the police or sheriff's department that originally arrested the person using your identity, or the court agency that issued the warrant for the arrest. File an impersonation report to confirm your identity. The police department may take a full set of your fingerprints and your photograph, and copies of any photo identification documents such as your driver's license, passport, or visa. They should compare the prints and photographs with those of the impostor to establish your innocence. If the arrest warrant is from a state or county other than where you live, ask your local police department to send the impersonation report to the police department in the jurisdiction where the arrest warrant, traffic citation, or criminal conviction originated.

The law enforcement agency should then recall any warrants and issue a "clearance letter" or certificate of release (if you were arrested/booked). You'll need to keep this document with you at all times in case you're wrongly arrested. Also, ask the law enforcement agency to file, with the district attorney's (D.A.) office and/or court where the crime took place, the record of the follow-up investigation establishing your innocence. This will result in an amended complaint being issued. Once your name is recorded in a criminal database, it's unlikely that it will be completely removed from the official record. Ask that the "key name," or "primary name," be changed from your name to the impostor's name (or to "John Doe" if the impostor's true identity is not known), with your name noted only as an alias.

You'll also want to clear your name in the court records. You'll need to determine which state law(s) will help you do this, and how. If your state has no formal procedure for clearing your record, contact the D.A.'s office in the county where the case was originally prosecuted. Ask the D.A.'s office for the appropriate court records needed to clear your name.

Finally, contact your state DMV to find out if your driver's license is being used by the identity thief. Ask that your files be flagged for possible fraud.

You may need to hire a criminal defense attorney to help you clear your name. Contact Legal Services in your state or your local bar association for help in finding an attorney.

Driver's License

What do I do if the identity thief has gotten a driver's license in my name? If you think your name or SSN is being used by an identity thief to get a driver's license or a nondriver's ID card, contact your DMV. If your state uses your SSN as your driver's license number, ask to substitute another number.

Investment Transactions

What do I do about investment transactions made in my name? The U.S. Securities and Exchange Commission's (SEC) Office of Investor Education and Assistance serves investors who complain to the SEC about investment fraud or the mishandling of their investments by securities professionals. If you believe that an identity thief has tampered with your securities investments or a brokerage account, immediately report it to your broker or account manager and to the SEC. You can file a complaint with the SEC using the online Complaint Center at: www.sec.gov/complaints.html.

Be sure to include as much detail as possible. If you don't have access to the Internet, you can write to the SEC at: SEC Office of Investor Education and Assistance,

450 Fifth Street, NW, Washington, DC 20549-0213. For general questions, call 202-942-7040. For general information: www.sec.gov.

Stolen Mail or Fraudulent Changes of Address

The U.S. Postal Inspection Service (USPIS) is the law enforcement arm of the U.S. Postal Service and is responsible for investigating cases of identity theft. USPIS has primary jurisdiction in all matters infringing on the integrity of the U.S. mail. If an identity thief has stolen your mail to get new credit cards, bank or credit card statements, prescreened credit offers, or tax information; has falsified change-of-address forms; or has obtained your personal information through a fraud conducted by mail, report it to your local postal inspector. You can locate the USPIS district office nearest you by calling your local post office or checking the list at www.usps.gov/websites/depart/inspect.

Telephone Service

What do I do if the thief has obtained phone service in my name?   If an identity thief has established phone service in your name, is making unauthorized calls that seem to come from—and are billed to—your cellular phone, or is using your calling card and PIN, contact your service provider immediately to cancel the account and/or calling card. Open new accounts and choose new PINs. If you're having trouble getting fraudulent phone charges removed from your account or getting an unauthorized account closed, contact the appropriate agency as noted below:

For local service, contact your state Public Utility Commission, listed in the Blue Pages of your telephone directory.

For cellular phones and long distance, contact the Federal Communications Commission (FCC), at www.fcc.gov. The FCC regulates interstate and international communications by radio, television, wire, satellite, and cable. You can contact the FCC's Consumer Information Bureau to find information about forms, applications, and current issues before the FCC. Call: 1-888-CALL-FCC; TTY: 1-888-TELL-FCC, or write: Federal Communications Commission, Consumer Information Bureau, 445 12th Street, SW, Room 5A863, Washington, DC 20554. You can file complaints via the online complaint form at www.fcc.gov/cgb/complaints.html, or email questions to fccinfo@fcc.gov.

Student Loan

What do I do if the thief has used my identity to take out a student loan?   Contact the school or program that opened the student loan to close the loan. At the same time, report the fraudulent loan to the U.S. Department of Education.

Call: Inspector General's Hotline at 1-800-MIS-USED

Online: www.ed.gov/offices/OIG/hotline.htm

Write: Office of Inspector General

        U.S. Department of Education

        400 Maryland Avenue, SW

        Washington, DC 20202-1510

Tax Returns

What do I do if the thief is using my identity to file tax returns?   The Internal Revenue Service (IRS) (www.treas.gov/irs/ci) is responsible for administering and enforcing tax laws. If you believe someone has assumed your identity to file federal income tax returns, or to commit other tax fraud, call toll-free: 1-800-829-0433. Victims of identity theft who are having trouble filing their returns should call the IRS Taxpayer Advocates Office, toll-free: 1-877-777-4778.

What should I do if I've done everything you've advised, and I am still having problems?   There are cases where victims do everything right and still spend years dealing with problems related to identity theft. The good news is that most victims can get their cases resolved by being vigilant, assertive, and organized. Don't procrastinate on contacting companies to address the problems. Don't be afraid to go up the chain of command or make complaints, if necessary. Keep organized files. If you haven't filed a complaint with the FTC or updated it, you should do so and provide details of the problems that you are having. You also can call the FTC hotline (1-877-IDTHEFT) to talk with one of our counselors, or, for individual counseling, contact one of the nonprofit victim associations listed in Helpful Links on the FTC Website. If your problems are stemming from a failure of a party to perform its legal obligations, you may want to consult an attorney who specializes in such violations. Contact Legal Services in your state or your local bar association for help in finding an attorney.

Phishing

Internet scammers casting about for people's financial information have a new way to lure unsuspecting victims; they go "phishing." Phishing is a high-tech scam that uses spam to deceive consumers into disclosing their credit card numbers, bank account information, Social Security numbers, passwords, and other sensitive personal information.

According to the Federal Trade Commission, the latest phishing scam involves emails that claim to be from regulations.gov, a website where consumers can participate in government rule making by submitting comments. The emails' subject lines typically read "Official information" or "Urgent information to all credit card holders!" The message's text claims, "Due to recent changes in Rules and Regulations, it is required by Law for all Internet users to identify themselves in compliance with Federal Regulations to create a secure and safer Internet community." The email includes a link to a website that mimics regulations.gov and asks readers to provide their personal and financial information.

If you get an unsolicited email that claims to be from the federal government and asks for your information, do not respond. Send the spam to the FTC at uce@ftc.gov so that it can be available to law enforcement.

Avoid emailing personal and financial information. If you get an unexpected email from a company or government agency asking for your personal information, contact the company or agency cited in the email, using a telephone number you know to be genuine, or start a new Internet session and type in the Web address that you know is correct.

If you have recently shared your credit card or bank account information in response to an unsolicited email that claimed to be from regulations.gov, you should notify your credit card company or bank immediately and discuss whether you should cancel your accounts. In any event, you should carefully monitor your accounts. If you provided your Social Security number, you should contact one of the three national consumer reporting agencies, ask that a fraud alert be placed on your accounts, and obtain copies of your credit reports. You also should visit the FTC's Identity Theft Website (www.consumer.gov/idtheft) to file a complaint and learn more about how to minimize your risk of damage from identity theft.

Regulations.gov is operated by the United States Environmental Protection Agency in association with the Food and Drug Administration, the National Archives and Records Administration/Office of the Federal Register, and the Government Printing Office. The FTC and other federal agencies use the regulations.gov portal to receive comments from the public regarding proposed rules and regulations.

The FTC works for the consumer to prevent fraudulent, deceptive, and unfair business practices in the marketplace and to provide information to help consumers spot, stop, and avoid them. To file a complaint or to get free information on consumer issues, visit www.ftc.gov or call toll-free: 1-877-FTC-HELP (1-877-382-4357); TTY: 1-866-653-4261. The FTC enters Internet, telemarketing, identity theft, and other fraud-related complaints into Consumer Sentinel, a secure, online database available to hundreds of civil and criminal law enforcement agencies in the U.S. and abroad.

A Few Travel Tips

It is wise to always be vigilant when protecting one's identity, but diligence is particularly important when traveling, because thieves frequent airports and case hotel lobbies, targeting unsuspecting travelers.

A few points to keep in mind:

1. Don't take personal checks; take traveler's checks, which are very safe.

2. If you must take personal checks, open up a second checking account, with as low a balance as possible and no automatic advance or line of credit. This greatly reduces your potential exposure.

3. Never have your full name imprinted on your checks; use your initials.

4. Never have your home address imprinted on your check. Imprint your post office box.

5. Remember to take your backup information with you, as noted earlier:

   ➤ Credit card numbers and telephone numbers to report lost or stolen cards
   ➤ Bank account numbers, branch telephone number, and after-hours telephone number to report fraud
   ➤ Important insurance numbers
   ➤ Copy of your driver's license
   ➤ Names, addresses, and telephone numbers of the three major credit bureaus
   ➤ Names and telephone numbers of the major check approval services

6. Take a second photo ID such as a passport. Remember that positive photo ID is *required* to board an airplane.

7. Carry your physician's name and telephone number.

Internal Control Analysis, Documentation, and Recommendations for Improvement

THE PURPOSE OF this section and the companion website is to thoroughly analyze, document, and communicate recommendations for improvements to CPAs' audit work papers and internal audit committee documents.

Additionally, this section has been designed to assist auditors complying with the requirements of Statement of Auditing Standard No. 99.

Although every attempt has been made to be as thorough as possible, obviously not every situation or issue can be foreseen, so it is incumbent upon CPAs and internal auditors to expand the scope of this section as applicable under the circumstances.

Firm Information

Client_____

Audit Dates _____

In-Charge Accountant _____
Work Telephone_____
Emergency Telephone _____

Accounting Assistants:

Name _____

Work Telephone _____

Emergency Telephone _____

Name _____

Work Telephone _____

Emergency Telephone _____

Name _____

Work Telephone _____

Emergency Telephone _____

Name _____

Work Telephone _____

Emergency Telephone _____

Name _____

Work Telephone _____

Emergency Telephone _____

Name _____

Work Telephone _____

Emergency Telephone _____

Name _____

Work Telephone _____

Emergency Telephone _____

Name _____

Work Telephone _____

Emergency Telephone _____

Client Information

Note: If the client is a not-for-profit organization, proceed to the Not-for-Profit Organizations: Elected Leadership section that immediately follows this section.

Client _____

Address _____

_____

_____

Telephone Number _____

Type of Entity _____

Federal ID Number _____

Board of Directors:

Name

Chairman of the Board _____

President _____

Treasurer _____

Secretary _____

Vice Presidents:

_____

_____

_____

_____

Other Board Positions:

_____   _____

_____   _____

_____   _____

Key Staff:

Name

Chief Executive Officer _____

Chief Operating Officer _____

Chief Financial Officer _____

Controller _____

Other Key Staff Positions:

_____   _____

_____   _____

_____   _____

Not–for–Profit Organizations: Elected Leadership

Note the names and contact information of the organization's executive committees, if applicable:

Chief Elected Officer:

Title	Name	Contact Information
_____	_____	_____
		_____
		_____
		_____

Treasurer:

Name	Contact Information
_____	_____
	_____
	_____
	_____

Corporate Secretary:

Name	Contact Information
_____	_____
	_____
	_____
	_____

Other Executive Committee Members:

Title	Name	Contact Information
_____	_____	_____
		_____
		_____
		_____
_____	_____	_____
		_____
		_____
		_____
_____	_____	_____
		_____
		_____
		_____
_____	_____	_____
		_____
		_____
		_____
_____	_____	_____
		_____
		_____
		_____
_____	_____	_____
		_____
		_____
		_____

Note titles and names of other board of director members:

Title	Name	Contact Information
_____	_____	_____
		_____
		_____
		_____
_____	_____	_____
		_____
		_____
		_____
_____	_____	_____
		_____
		_____
		_____
_____	_____	_____
		_____
		_____
		_____
_____	_____	_____
		_____
		_____
		_____
_____	_____	_____
		_____
		_____
		_____
_____	_____	_____
		_____
		_____
		_____
_____	_____	_____
		_____
		_____
		_____

Note the contact information for the current Budget and Finance Committee, if applicable:

Chairman:

Name	Contact Information
_____	_____
	_____
	_____
	_____

Committee Members:

Name	Contact Information
_____	_____
	_____
	_____
	_____
_____	_____
	_____
	_____
	_____
_____	_____
	_____
	_____
	_____
_____	_____
	_____
	_____
	_____
_____	_____
	_____
	_____
	_____

Note the contact information for the Internal Audit Committee, if applicable:

Chairman:

<table>
<tr><td>Name</td><td>Contact Information</td></tr>
<tr><td>_____</td><td>_____</td></tr>
<tr><td></td><td>_____</td></tr>
<tr><td></td><td>_____</td></tr>
<tr><td></td><td>_____</td></tr>
</table>

Committee Members:

<table>
<tr><td>Name</td><td>Contact Information</td></tr>
<tr><td>_____</td><td>_____</td></tr>
<tr><td></td><td>_____</td></tr>
<tr><td></td><td>_____</td></tr>
<tr><td></td><td>_____</td></tr>
<tr><td>_____</td><td>_____</td></tr>
<tr><td></td><td>_____</td></tr>
<tr><td></td><td>_____</td></tr>
<tr><td></td><td>_____</td></tr>
<tr><td>_____</td><td>_____</td></tr>
<tr><td></td><td>_____</td></tr>
<tr><td></td><td>_____</td></tr>
<tr><td></td><td>_____</td></tr>
<tr><td>_____</td><td>_____</td></tr>
<tr><td></td><td>_____</td></tr>
<tr><td></td><td>_____</td></tr>
<tr><td></td><td>_____</td></tr>
</table>

Are there any other committees or individuals among the membership that have financial responsibilities, such as an investment committee, insurance committee, long-range planning committee, etc.?

Yes   No

____   ____

If yes, note detail and contact information accordingly:

_____

_____

_____

_____

_____

_____

_____

_____

_____

_____

_____

_____

_____

_____

_____

_____

_____

_____

_____

_____

_____

_____

_____

_____

_____

_____

_____

_____

Finance and Accounting Staffing

Objective: To document finance/accounting organization and staffing, and to assess competence.

Name

Chief Financial Officer

_____

Controller

_____

General Ledger Accountants:

Position   Name

_____   _____

_____   _____

_____   _____

Accounts Receivable Accountants:

Position   Name

_____   _____

_____   _____

_____   _____

Accounts Payable Accountants:

Position   Name

_____   _____

_____   _____

_____   _____

Payroll Accountants:

Position   Name

_____   _____

_____   _____

_____   _____

Inventory Accountants:

Position   Name

_____   _____

_____   _____

_____   _____

Other Accounting/Financial Staff:

Position	Name
_____	_____
_____	_____
_____	_____
_____	_____
_____	_____
_____	_____

➤ Does the organization have formal job
descriptions for all accounting/finance/
staff positions?

    Yes   No   N/A

    _____ _____ _____

Comments:_____

_____

_____

_____

_____

➤ Does current accounting/financial staff
have the proper education, background,
and experience for their duties?

    Yes   No   N/A

    _____ _____ _____

Comments:_____

_____

_____

_____

_____

➤ Does it appear that the organization's current
staffing in accounting/finance is reasonable
considering the current workload?

    Yes   No   N/A

    _____ _____ _____

Comments:_____

_____

_____

_____

_____

➤ Does the organization conduct adequate
background checks on all accounting/
finance staff?

    Yes   No   N/A

    _____ _____ _____

Comments:_____

_____

_____

_____

_____

➤ Is training for new accounting/
finance staff adequate?

Yes   No   N/A

_____ _____ _____

Comments: _____

_____

_____

_____

_____

➤ Are accounting/finance staff
evaluated regularly?

Yes   No   N/A

_____ _____ _____

Comments: _____

_____

_____

_____

_____

➤ Does the organization have written
accounting/financial policies and
procedures?

Yes   No   N/A

_____ _____ _____

Comments: _____

_____

_____

_____

_____

➤ Does the organization have a current
chart of accounts?

Yes   No   N/A

_____ _____ _____

Comments: _____

_____

_____

_____

_____

➤ After review of finance/accounting staffing and other issues, comment on any deficiencies noted and recommendations for improvement:

_____

_____

_____

_____

_____

_____

_____

_____

_____

_____

_____

_____

_____

_____

_____

_____

_____

_____

_____

_____

_____

_____

_____

_____

_____

_____

_____

_____

_____

_____

_____

Internal Audit Committee

➤ Does the organization have written
policies and procedures for Internal
Audit Committee responsibilities?

Yes No N/A

_____ _____ _____

Comments: _____

_____

_____

_____

_____

Chairman:

   Name   Contact Information

_____ _____

            _____

            _____

            _____

Committee Members:

   Name   Contact Information

_____ _____

            _____

            _____

            _____

_____ _____

            _____

            _____

            _____

_____ _____

            _____

            _____

            _____

_____ _____

            _____

            _____

            _____

Name	Contact Information
_____	_____
	_____
	_____
	_____
_____	_____
	_____
	_____
_____	_____
	_____
	_____
_____	_____
	_____
	_____
_____	_____
	_____
	_____
_____	_____
	_____
	_____
_____	_____
	_____
	_____
	_____

Risk Assessment and Understanding the Entity

Objective: To ensure that SAS 99 requirements regarding understanding the client's business are met and documented.

➤ List action taken and resources obtained to ensure adequate understanding of the client's business:

_____

_____

_____

_____

_____

After ensuring proper understanding of the nature of the organization's business, comment on any issues noted and record recommendations for improvement:

_____

_____

_____

_____

_____

_____

_____

_____

_____

➤ Are any of the organization's line items
out of line, considering past history,   Yes   No   N/A
comparable organizations, etc.?   _____   _____   _____

If yes, what analytical action was taken to determine if fraud may be present, and what follow-up action was performed?

_____

_____

_____

_____

Brainstorming Sessions/Employee Interviews

Objective: SAS 99 requires CPA audit team members to meet and brainstorm concerning client fraud risk and internal control weaknesses, and to decide which client employees to interview and what interview questions to ask. While not required, this practice should be considered by internal audit committees, etc.

➤ Names and titles of brainstorming committee members:

Name	Title
_____	_____
_____	_____
_____	_____
_____	_____

➤ Date of meeting_____

➤ Summarize all perceived internal control weaknesses discussed and recommendations for improvement:

_____

_____

_____

_____

_____

➤ Names and titles of employees to be interviewed:

Name	Title
_____	_____
_____	_____
_____	_____
_____	_____

➤ Specific interview questions:

   ➤ Is the organization's Conflict of Interest policy clear and understandable?

   ➤ Is the organization's Conditions of Employment agreement clear and understandable?

   ➤ Are you aware of the existence of fraud, conflicts of interest, or unethical behavior?

   ➤ Are you aware of any potential for fraud, conflicts of interest, or unethical behavior?

   ➤ Has any employee ever approached you to conspire in fraud, conflicts of interest, or unethical behavior?

   ➤ Has anyone outside the organization ever approached you to conspire in fraud, conflicts of interest, or unethical behavior?

   ➤ Are you aware of any weaknesses in internal controls that could lead to fraud?

   ➤ Are the controls over confidential customer information (credit card numbers, bank account numbers, etc.) adequate?

   ➤ Are controls over confidential employee personnel records adequate?

   ➤ Is the organization policy for reporting suspicious behavior to the appropriate level of management clear and understandable?

   ➤ Is the organization's whistleblower protection policy clear and understandable?

   ➤ Do you have any suggestions for improvement for the organization taken as a whole?

   ➤ Does the organization employ family members with direct authority over other family members?

   ➤ Are you aware of any interpersonal relationships that could lead to weak internal controls?

Other questions as determined by the committee:

_____

_____

_____

_____

_____

Results of Interviews:

The staff interviews and results should be written and included with the audit work papers.

After the interviews, the results should be discussed among audit team members who have the responsibility of analyzing the risks and formulating a plan of action.

➤ Note specific areas of concern resulting from staff interviews:

_____

_____

_____

_____

_____

➤ Detail plan of action formulated to investigate areas of concern:

_____

_____

_____

_____

_____

➤ Summarize results of implementing the plan of action, and further action warranted, if necessary:

_____

_____

_____

_____

_____

➤ Comment on any brainstorming session or employee interview issues that need addressing, and record recommendations for improvement:

_____

_____

_____

_____

_____

_____

_____

_____

_____

_____

_____

General Internal Control Environment

Objective: To review the overall internal control environment and assess risk factors and recommendations for improvement.

➤ Does the organization have an effective and written policy whereby all employees are required to report on any suspected illegal or unethical activity to the appropriate level of management in an anonymous manner?

    Yes   No   N/A

    ____   ____   ____

Comments: _____

_____

_____

_____

_____

➤ Does the organization have a written whistle-blower protection policy?

    Yes   No   N/A

    ____   ____   ____

Comments: _____

_____

_____

_____

_____

➤ Does the organization certify its financial statement in accordance with Sarbanes/Oxley?

    Yes   No   N/A

    ____   ____   ____

Comments: _____

_____

_____

_____

_____

➤ If the organization does certify its financial statements, note titles and names of signers:

Title   Name

_____   _____

_____   _____

_____   _____

_____   _____

➤ Does the organization have a written   Yes   No   N/A
  code of ethics for financial management?   ____   ____   ____

  Comments:_____

  _____

  _____

  _____

  _____

➤ Has the organization experienced a material   Yes   No
  fraud or embezzlement in the past?   ____   ____
  If yes, document this incident and comment on effectiveness of follow-up
  action:

  _____

  _____

  _____

  _____

  _____

➤ Is the organization's management suspicious
  of any employee dishonesty, or any illegal or   Yes   No
  unethical activity?   ____   ____
  If yes, document the concerns, follow-up procedures, and results:

  _____

  _____

  _____

  _____

➤ Have Management Letters been issued
  for any of the prior three years with regard   Yes   No
  to internal control issues?   _____   _____

  If yes, comment on issues and effectiveness of follow-up procedures and
  results:

  _____

  _____

  _____

  _____

  _____

➤ Has the organization had any independent
  studies of the internal control environment   Yes   No
  conducted during any of the last three years?   _____   _____

  If yes, comment on any issues and effectiveness of follow-up procedures and
  results:

  _____

  _____

  _____

  _____

  _____

➤ Does it appear that management and staff
  conduct their business dealing with integrity   Yes   No
  in all aspects?   _____   _____

  Comments: _____

  _____

  _____

  _____

  _____

➤ Does the organization have written internal   Yes   No
  control policies and procedures?   _____   _____

Comments: _____

_____

_____

_____

_____

➤ Does management take appropriate
action for departures from established   Yes   No
policies and procedures?   _____   _____

Comments: _____

_____

_____

_____

_____

➤ Are there any personal relationships among
employees or any conflicts of interest that may   Yes   No
compromise the integrity of internal controls?   _____   _____

Comments: _____

_____

_____

_____

_____

➤ After the general internal control environment has been evaluated, summarize
material weaknesses noted and record recommendations for improvement:

_____

_____

_____

_____

_____

_____

_____

_____

_____

CPA Financial Statements, Management Letters, and Consulting Agreements

Financial Statements

Note the CPA firm(s) that have conducted business with the organization over the past three years:

Year(s): _____

Name of Firm: _____

Address: _____

_____

_____

Primary Contact: _____

Telephone: _____

Email: _____

Website: _____

List the types of service(s) that the firm provided (audit, review, compilation, tax return preparation, consulting, agreed upon procedures, etc.):

_____

_____

_____

_____

_____

If the organization has a relationship with a CPA firm, did it receive:

	Yes	No
An audit	_____	_____
A review	_____	_____
A compilation	_____	_____
Consulting services	_____	_____

If the organization received an audit, what type of audit opinion did it receive for the last three years:

	Unqualified	Qualified	Adverse	Disclaimer
Year 1	_____	_____	_____	_____
Year 2	_____	_____	_____	_____
Year 3	_____	_____	_____	_____

If the organization received other than an unqualified opinion for any of the past three years, note the type of opinion received, reason, follow-up by board and key staff, any issue(s) that continue to be unresolved, and current status recommendations to resolve issue(s) accordingly:

_____

_____

_____

_____

_____

_____

_____

_____

_____

_____

_____

Management Letters

➤ Did the organization receive a CPA Management Letter for any of the last three years?

Yes _____ No _____

If yes, are copies included in this report?

Yes _____ No _____

If no, explain why Management Letters are unavailable:

_____

_____

_____

_____

_____

➤ Did a representative of the CPA firm
present the Management Letter to the   Yes   No
board of directors?
                                                       _____   _____

If no, how was the Management Letter handled by the CPA firm?

_____

_____

_____

_____

_____

➤ Has the board of directors thoroughly
discussed Management Letter issues and   Yes   No
ensured that issues were resolved?
                                                       _____   _____

If no, explain:

_____

_____

_____

_____

_____

➤ Note any unresolved Management Letter issues and appropriate recommendations:

_____

_____

_____

_____

_____

Consulting Agreements

If the organization entered into any consulting arrangements with any CPA firm
over the past three years, note the following:

Year _____ Firm_____

Description of consulting services contracted for, including fees:

_____

_____

_____

_____

_____

_____

_____

_____

_____

_____

_____

_____

_____

_____

_____

_____

_____

_____

_____

_____

_____

_____

_____

_____

_____

_____

_____

_____

_____

_____

Related-Party Transactions

Objective: To ensure that the existence of any related-party transactions is fully documented and disclosed adequately.

➤ Does the organization have any long-term debt instruments with owners, directors, employees, or any other individuals with ties to the organization?

Yes   No

_____   _____

If yes, fully detail the arrangement, including individual's name, relationship with the organization, type of debt instrument, interest rate, verification that tax ramifications have been handled properly, etc.:

_____

_____

_____

_____

_____

Comment on any issues surrounding related-party transactions, and record recommendations for improvement:

Nepotism

Objective: To ensure that there is an adequate segregation of responsibilities and authority between family members working within the organization.

➤ Are there any family members working   Yes   No
  within the organization?   ____   ____

  If yes, note the names, titles, and relationship:

  Name   Title   Relationship

  _____   _____   _____

  _____   _____   _____

  _____   _____   _____

  _____   _____   _____

  _____   _____   _____

➤ Is there an adequate segregation of
  responsibilities and authority between   Yes   No
  family members?   ____   ____

  If no, comment on the disparity, and document that the issue has been brought
  to the attention of the appropriate level of management:

  _____

  _____

  _____

  _____

  _____

Comment on any other nepotism issue and record recommendations for
improvement:

_____

_____

_____

_____

_____

_____

_____

_____

_____

Conflicts of Interest (Excluding Nepotism)

Objective: To ensure that real or perceived conflicts of interest are brought to the attention of the appropriate level of management.

➤ Does the organization have a Conflicts
of Interest policy and form, and has it
been signed by individuals on the board   Yes   No
of directors?   _____   _____

Comments: _____

_____

_____

_____

_____

➤ Does the organization have a Conflicts
of Interest policy and form, and has it
been signed by all employees, including   Yes   No
key management positions?   _____   _____

Comments: _____

_____

_____

_____

_____

Comment on any existing conflicts of interest, and document that they have been
communicated to the attention of the appropriate level of management:

_____

_____

_____

_____

_____

_____

_____

_____

_____

_____

Comment on any board of director, employee, or outside vendor relationships that may be perceived as a conflict of interest:

_____

_____

_____

_____

_____

_____

_____

_____

_____

_____

_____

_____

_____

Comment on any conflict-of-interest issues that should be communicated to the organization, and record possible recommendations for improvement:

_____

_____

_____

_____

_____

_____

_____

_____

_____

_____

_____

_____

_____

_____

_____

_____

_____

_____

Accounting and Financial Policies and Procedures Manual

Objective: To ensure that accounting and financial policies and procedures are documented, are in accordance with GAAP and current tax laws, and are followed consistently.

Additionally, these policies and procedures should be clear and understandable such that a competent substitute accountant could manage the organization's financial function in the event of an emergency, employee terminations, etc.

➤ Does the organization have a written accounting   Yes   No   N/A
and financial policies and procedures manual?   ___   ___   ___

Comments: _____

_____

_____

_____

_____

➤ Are accounting and financial policies
reasonable and in accordance with   Yes   No   N/A
prevailing GAAP and tax law?   ___   ___   ___

Comments: _____

_____

_____

_____

_____

Comment on your assessment of financial and accounting policies and procedures, and record recommendations for improvement:

_____

_____

_____

_____

_____

_____

_____

_____

Journal Entries

Objective: To ensure that journal entry procedures are documented, reasonable, and approved and reviewed by the appropriate level of management.

➤ Describe journal entry request and approval procedures:

_____

_____

_____

_____

_____

➤ Comment on any journal entry request and approval procedures that are insufficient and recommendations for improvement:

_____

_____

_____

_____

_____

➤ Do all journal entries require full explanations?   Yes   No

                                                       _____   _____

Comments:_____

_____

_____

_____

_____

➤ What positions have authority to request journal entries?

Name	Title
_____	_____
_____	_____
_____	_____
_____	_____

Comments: _____

_____

_____

_____

_____

➤ What positions have journal entry approval authority?

Name	Title
_____	_____
_____	_____
_____	_____
_____	_____
_____	_____

Comments: _____

_____

_____

_____

_____

➤ Is there adequate segregation between individuals authorized to approve journal entries and the following functions?

	Yes	No	N/A
Cash disbursements	___	___	___
Cash receipts	___	___	___
Bank reconciliations	___	___	___
Accounts receivable	___	___	___
Petty cash disbursements	___	___	___
Payroll	___	___	___
Employee benefits	___	___	___
Revenue recognition	___	___	___
Expense recognition	___	___	___
Depreciation calculations	___	___	___
Amortization calculations	___	___	___
Customer credit	___	___	___
Write-off authority	___	___	___
Inventory adjustments	___	___	___
Employee loans	___	___	___

Travel advances   _____   _____   _____
Other:

_____   _____   _____   _____

_____   _____   _____   _____

_____   _____   _____   _____

Comment on any journal entry procedures that are deficient, and record recommendations for improvement:

_____

_____

_____

_____

_____

_____

_____

_____

_____

_____

_____

_____

_____

_____

Management Overrides

Objective: Every organization will experience situations in which exceptions to established accounting and financial policies and procedures are warranted. It is crucially important to ensure that management overrides are documented, have been approved by the appropriate level of management, and do not result in fake or misleading financial statement, personal gain, etc.

➤ What positions have authority to approve deviations from established accounting and financial policies and procedures?

Name	Title
_____	_____
_____	_____
_____	_____
_____	_____
_____	_____

Comment on any weaknesses in management override procedures, and record recommendations for improvement:

_____

_____

_____

_____

_____

_____

_____

_____

_____

_____

_____

_____

_____

Cash and Cash Equivalents (Excluding Petty Cash)

Objective: To ensure that cash and cash equivalents are secure, classified properly, and earning optimal interest.

➤ Note all organization disbursing accounts:

Bank	Type of Account	Account Number	Interest Rate

Comments: _____

_____

_____

_____

_____

➤ Note all organization savings accounts:

Bank	Type of Account	Account Number	Interest Rate

Comments: _____

_____

_____

_____

_____

➤ If the organization has cash registers, note the location and amount of each bank:

Location	Amount of Bank
_____	$ _____
_____	_____
_____	_____
_____	_____
_____	_____

➤ Are controls over cash register activity and access reasonable under the circumstances?

	Yes	No	N/A
	____	____	____

Comments and recommendations for improvement:

_____

_____

_____

_____

_____

➤ Note all organization certificates of deposit:

Bank	Certificate#	Purchase Date	Maturity Date	Interest
_____	_____	_____	_____	_____
_____	_____	_____	_____	_____
_____	_____	_____	_____	_____
_____	_____	_____	_____	_____
_____	_____	_____	_____	_____

Comments: _____

_____

_____

_____

_____

➤ Who is the custodian of certificates of deposit?:

Name _____ Title _____

Comments: _____

_____

_____

_____

_____

➤ Note any other types of cash and cash equivalent accounts and detailed description:

_____

_____

_____

_____

_____

Comments: _____

_____

_____

_____

_____

➤ Has the existence of all cash and cash   Yes   No   N/A
equivalent accounts been verified?   _____   _____   _____

Comments: _____

_____

_____

_____

Comment on any issues surrounding the handling of cash and cash equivalents, if not adequate, and record recommendations for improvement:

_____

_____

_____

_____

_____

_____

_____

Petty Cash

Objective: To ensure that the petty cash fund is reasonable, secured, and accounted for properly.

➢ Who is the petty cash custodian?

Name_____ Title_____

➢ What is the amount of the petty cash fund? $_____

➢ Where is the petty cash fund kept?

_____

_____

_____

➢ Describe the petty cash disbursement procedures:

_____

_____

_____

_____

_____

➢ Are employee loans from petty cash prohibited?   Yes   No   N/A
                                                    ____   ____   ____

Comments: _____

_____

_____

_____

_____

➤ Are procedures surrounding petty cash   Yes   No   N/A
  fund security and disbursements adequate?   _____   _____   _____

Comments: _____

_____

_____

_____

_____

Comment on any issues surrounding petty cash fund procedures, and record recommendations for improvement:

_____

_____

_____

_____

_____

_____

_____

_____

_____

_____

_____

_____

_____

_____

_____

_____

Receipts and Accounts Receivables

Objective: To ensure that controls surrounding receipts and accounts receivable are adequate, accounts receivable customer balances are monitored, and write-off procedures are adequate.

➤ Does the organization extend credit
to customers?

  Yes   No

  _____   _____

If yes, briefly comment on credit approval policies that are required before credit is extended:

_____

_____

_____

_____

_____

➤ Is the segregation of duties between
the billing functions and credit
functions adequate?

  Yes   No   N/A

  _____   _____   _____

Comments: _____

_____

_____

_____

_____

➤ Are accounts receivable balances
monitored adequately and routinely?

  Yes   No   N/A

  _____   _____   _____

Comments: _____

_____

_____

_____

_____

➤ Is the segregation of duties concerning the issuing of credit memos and billing adequate?

Yes ____   No ____   N/A ____

Comments: _____

_____

_____

_____

_____

➤ Is there adequate segregation of duties concerning the inventory custody, billing, shipping, cash sales, and accounts receivable functions?

Yes ____   No ____   N/A ____

Comments: _____

_____

_____

_____

_____

➤ Are customer complaints monitored and followed up by someone not associated with accounts receivable and receipt functions?

Yes ____   No ____   N/A ____

Comments: _____

_____

_____

_____

_____

➤ Is confidential customer information (credit card numbers, etc.) controlled adequately?

Yes ____   No ____   N/A ____

Comments: _____

_____

_____

_____

_____

➤ Is access to customer information and accounts   Yes   No   N/A
   receivable limited to a need-to-know basis?   _____   _____   _____

Comments: _____

_____

_____

_____

_____

➤ Are the accounts receivable aging reports   Yes   No   N/A
   adequate?   _____   _____   _____

Comments: _____

_____

_____

_____

_____

➤ Are customer statements reviewed and
   mailed out by someone not connected   Yes   No   N/A
   with accounts receivable?   _____   _____   _____

Comments: _____

_____

_____

_____

➤ Describe in detail the organization's accounts receivable write-off policy and
   comment on recommendations for improvement, if applicable:

_____

_____

_____

_____

_____

_____

_____

_____

_____

_____

_____

_____

Comment on any issues concerning the organization's handling of receipts and accounts receivable, and record recommendations for improvement:

_____

_____

_____

_____

_____

_____

_____

_____

_____

_____

_____

_____

_____

_____

_____

_____

_____

_____

_____

_____

_____

_____

_____

Disbursements

Objective: To ensure that all disbursements are legitimate, proper approvals have been obtained, supporting documentation is appropriate, security is enforced, and adequate segregation of responsibilities exists.

➤ Is the check supply under lock and key?   Yes   No
                                                   _____   _____

Comments: _____

_____

_____

_____

_____

➤ What positions have access to the check supply?

            Name   Title

_____   _____

_____   _____

_____   _____

_____   _____

_____   _____

Comments: _____

_____

_____

_____

_____

➤ **Important:** Does the organization utilize   Yes   No
a bank's Positive Pay service?   _____   _____

Note: Taking advantage of Positive Pay is crucially important. If the organization is not utilizing this vital service, document that using this service has been fully explained to the appropriate level of management, management's reaction, etc.:

_____

_____

_____

_____

_____

➤ Does the organization use nonscannable   Yes   No
  check stock?   _____   _____

  Comments: _____

  _____

  _____

  _____

  _____

➤ Are all individuals in the accounting
  and financial functions prohibited from   Yes   No
  signing checks?   _____   _____

  Comments: _____

  _____

  _____

  _____

  _____

➤ Is there adequate segregation of duties among
  check requests, check preparation, check signing, Yes   No
  mailing of checks, and bank reconciliations?   _____   _____

  Comments: _____

  _____

  _____

  _____

  _____

➤ Are two signatures required on all checks,   Yes   No
  regardless of the amount?   _____   _____

  Comments: _____

  _____

  _____

  _____

  _____

➤ **Important:** For work paper documentation and signature comparison purposes, have a member of the audit or internal audit team witness authorized check signers sign their signature as they would sign a check:

Signer's Name	Signer's Title	Signer's Signature
_____	_____	_____
_____	_____	_____
_____	_____	_____
_____	_____	_____
_____	_____	_____

Name, title, date, and signature of the audit or internal audit team member who witnessed check signature:

Name	Title	Date	Signature
_____	_____	_____	_____

Comments: _____

_____

_____

_____

_____

➤ Does the organization use a purchase   Yes   No
order system?   ____   ____

Comments: _____

_____

_____

_____

_____

➤ Is the current system of approving invoices   Yes   No
from vendors for payment adequate?   ____   ____

Comments: _____

_____

_____

_____

_____

➤ **Important:** As in the case of check signers, for work paper documentation and signature comparisons, have a member of the audit or internal audit team witness signatures of individuals authorized to approve purchase orders, invoices, etc.:

Approver's Name	Approver's Title	Approver's Signature
_____	_____	_____
_____	_____	_____
_____	_____	_____
_____	_____	_____
_____	_____	_____

Name, title, date, and signature of the audit or internal audit team who witnessed the authorized approver's signature:

Name	Title	Date	Signature
_____	_____	_____	_____

Comments: _____

_____

_____

_____

_____

Accounts Payable and Other Current Liabilities

Objective: To ensure that controls over disbursements are adequate and that current liabilities are recorded properly on the financial statements.

➤ Describe in detail procedures and approvals required before checks can be issued and recommendations for improvement:

_____

_____

_____

_____

_____

_____

_____

➤ Is there adequate segregation of responsibilities for approving invoices for payment and accounts payable?

Yes _____   No _____

Comments: _____

_____

_____

_____

_____

➤ Are individuals with invoice approval authority and accounts payable responsibilities required to take vacation, and do other individuals assume their responsibilities?

Yes _____   No _____

Comments: _____

_____

_____

_____

_____

➤ Is the check supply under lock and key?   Yes   No
                                                  _____   _____

Comments: _____

_____

_____

_____

_____

➤ Is access to the check supply on an   Yes   No
  "as needed" basis?   _____   _____

Comments: _____

_____

_____

_____

_____

➤ Comment in detail on existing procedures for voiding checks and recommendations for improvement:

_____

_____

_____

_____

_____

_____

_____

➤ Are checks voided by cutting off the   Yes   No
  signature line?   _____   _____

Comments: _____

_____

_____

_____

_____

➤ Are voided checks filed and accounted
for properly?

Yes _____ No _____

Comments: _____

_____

_____

_____

_____

➤ Is confidential vendor information (FIN, etc.)
safeguarded adequately?

Yes _____ No _____

Comments: _____

_____

_____

_____

_____

➤ Is access to accounts payable information
limited to a need-to-know basis?

Yes _____ No _____

Comments: _____

_____

_____

_____

_____

➤ Does the organization maintain
an Approved Vendor list?

Yes _____ No _____

Comments: _____

_____

_____

_____

_____

Comment on any accounts payable issues, and record recommendations for improvement:

_____

_____

_____

_____

_____

_____

_____

_____

_____

_____

_____

_____

_____

_____

_____

_____

_____

_____

Fidelity Bonds

➤ Does the organization have a Fidelity Bond? Yes No N/A

_____ _____ _____

If no, explain and record recommendations for improvement, if applicable:

_____

_____

_____

_____

_____

➤ If the organization has a Fidelity Bond, note the following:

Insurance company _____

Address _____

_____

Agent name _____

Telephone number _____

Emergency telephone number _____

Policy number _____

Amount of Bond $ _____

Deductible $ _____

➤ Is the amount of the bond adequate? Yes No N/A

_____ _____ _____

If no, explain and record recommendations for improvement, if applicable:

_____

_____

_____

_____

_____

➤ Are there any Fidelity Bond requirements
due to line of credit agreements, floor plans, Yes No N/A
grants, mortgages, notes, etc.?

_____ _____ _____

If yes, explain and record recommendations for improvement, if applicable:

_____

_____

_____

_____

➤ Are all employees who handle cash,
checks, and credit card transactions   Yes   No   N/A
included in the Fidelity Bond?   _____   _____   _____

If no, explain and record recommendations for improvement, if applicable:

_____

_____

_____

_____

_____

➤ Has it been explained to management
that corporate officers and directors are   Yes   No   N/A
excluded from Fidelity Bond coverage?   _____   _____   _____

Note details accordingly:

_____

_____

_____

_____

Comment on any specific Fidelity Bond issues that indicate coverage is not adequate or complete, and note recommendations for improvement:

_____

_____

_____

_____

_____

Bank and Credit Card Statements

Objective: To ensure that bank and credit card statements are reviewed by appropriate individuals not responsible for check preparation, etc.

➤ Are the original bank statements sent
directly to the organization's finance
department by the issuer for review?

      Yes   No

     _____   _____

If no, explain and record recommendations for improvement, if applicable:

_____

_____

_____

_____

_____

➤ List titles and names of employees responsible for reconciling bank statements, next to the account(s) they are responsible for:

Title	Name	Bank Account(s)
_____	_____	_____
_____	_____	_____
_____	_____	_____
_____	_____	_____
_____	_____	_____

➤ Are material checks that are noted as
outstanding on the prior year-end bank
statement reconciliations investigated
thoroughly (endorsement comparisons,
double payments, etc.) by either a member
of the CPA firm or Internal Audit Committee
before the start of the following year's audit?

      Yes   No

     _____   _____

If no, explain and record recommendations for improvement, if applicable:

_____

_____

_____

_____

➤ Are *copies* of bank statements mailed
by the issuer to a secured post office
box accessible only by the following?   Yes   No

  ➤ The CEO   _____   _____

  ➤ The treasurer   _____   _____

  ➤ Members of the Internal Audit Committee   _____   _____

If no, explain and record recommendations for improvement, if applicable:

_____

_____

_____

_____

_____

➤ Does the CEO, treasurer, or members
of the Internal Audit Committee examine
the fronts and backs of checks (either
original checks, copies, or online images)
and investigate the following?   Yes   No

  ➤ Signature authenticity   _____   _____

  ➤ Out-of-sequence check numbers   _____   _____

  ➤ New vendors   _____   _____

  ➤ Unusual or large amounts   _____   _____

  ➤ Unusual endorsement stamps   _____   _____

If no, explain and record recommendations for improvement, if applicable:

_____

_____

_____

_____

_____

➤ Note all employees who have been issued credit cards: N/A
_____

Name	Title	Card Type	Account No. (Last 4 Digits)	Card Maximum
_____	_____	_____	_____	$ _____
_____	_____	_____	_____	_____
_____	_____	_____	_____	_____
_____	_____	_____	_____	_____
_____	_____	_____	_____	_____

➤ Are original credit card statements mailed directly to the organization's finance department for review and processing?

Yes _____   No _____   N/A _____

If no, explain and record recommendations for improvement, if applicable:

_____

_____

_____

_____

_____

➤ Describe the process for approving credit card transactions for payment: N/A
_____

_____

_____

_____

_____

_____

➤ Are the controls surrounding approving credit card transactions adequate under the circumstances?

Yes _____   No _____   N/A _____

If no, explain and record recommendations for improvement, if applicable:

_____

_____

_____

_____

_____

➤ Are *copies* of credit card statements mailed
  by the issuer to a secured post office box
  accessible only by the following?   Yes   No   N/A

  ➤ The CEO   _____   _____   _____

  ➤ The treasurer   _____   _____

  ➤ Members of the Internal Audit Committee   _____   _____

If no, explain and record recommendations for improvement, if applicable:

_____

_____

_____

_____

_____

➤ Do the CEO, treasurer, or members of the
  Internal Audit Committee examine employee
  credit card statements and investigate any   Yes   No   N/A
  suspicious transactions?   _____   _____   _____

If no, explain and record recommendations for improvement, if applicable:

_____

_____

_____

_____

_____

➤ Are employees who have been issued
organization credit cards aware of immediate
steps to take to report lost or stolen cards?

Yes   No   N/A

_____   _____   _____

If no, explain and record recommendations for improvement, if applicable:

_____

_____

_____

_____

_____

➤ If the organization reimburses employees
for purchases made on behalf of the
organization, are controls adequate?

Yes   No   N/A

_____   _____   _____

If no, explain and record recommendations for improvement, if applicable:

_____

_____

_____

_____

_____

Comment on any specific bank statement or credit card statement issues that indicate that controls are not adequate, with recommendations for improvement:

_____

_____

_____

_____

_____

_____

Inventory (Balances and Cost of Goods Sold)

Objective: To ensure that inventory acquisitions are handled properly, controls over inventory are sufficient, the inventory valuation method is reasonable and followed consistently, and periodic inventory counts are conducted properly.

➤ Does the organization capitalize inventory?   Yes   No   N/A

         _____   _____   _____

If yes, comment on the type of inventory capitalized:

_____

_____

_____

_____

_____

➤ Note titles and names of individuals with direct inventory responsibilities:

Name

Manager   _____

Other positions:

_____   _____

_____   _____

_____

➤ Does the organization have an inventory   Yes   No   N/A
   acquisition budget?   _____   _____   _____

Comments:_____

_____

_____

_____

➤ Describe inventory acquisition policies and procedures, with comments, if applicable:

_____

_____

_____

_____

_____

➤ What inventory valuation method(s) are used?

_____

_____

_____

_____

_____

➤ How often are inventories physically counted and compared to general ledger balances?

Comments: _____

_____

_____

_____

_____

➤ Have adequate background checks been conducted on employees who have access to inventory?

Yes   No   N/A

_____   _____   _____

Comments: _____

_____

_____

_____

_____

➤ Are employees who have access to   Yes   No   N/A
   inventory bonded?   _____   _____   _____

Comments:_____

_____

_____

_____

_____

➤ Are the controls over inventory adequate?   Yes   No   N/A

                                             _____   _____   _____

Comments:_____

_____

_____

_____

_____

➤ Is insurance over inventory values adequate?   Yes   No   N/A

                                             _____   _____   _____

Comments:_____

_____

_____

_____

_____

➤ Does the organization monitor inventory
   movement to ensure that slow-moving,
   defective, or obsolete inventory items are   Yes   No   N/A
   identified and accounted for properly?   _____   _____   _____

Comments:_____

_____

_____

_____

_____

➣ Are subsidiary inventory records accurate,
current, and compared to general ledger   Yes   No   N/A
balances routinely?   _____   _____   _____

Comments: _____

_____

_____

_____

_____

➣ Is access to inventory on an "as needed" basis?   Yes   No   N/A

                                                    _____   _____   _____

Comments: _____

_____

_____

_____

_____

➣ Are employees with inventory responsibilities
required to take vacations, and do other   Yes   No   N/A
employees assume their responsibilities?   _____   _____   _____

Comments: _____

_____

_____

_____

_____

➣ Does the organization employ "secret shoppers"   Yes   No   N/A
to test that sales are recorded properly?   _____   _____   _____

Comments: _____

_____

_____

_____

_____

➤ If the organization has inventory at remote   Yes   No   N/A
locations, are controls sufficient?   _____   _____   _____

Comments:_____

_____

_____

_____

_____

➤ If the organization has any inventory on   Yes   No   N/A
consignment, are controls adequate?   _____   _____   _____

Comments:_____

_____

_____

_____

_____

➤ Does Cost of Goods Sold appear reasonable   Yes   No   N/A
in relation to sales?   _____   _____   _____

Comments:_____

_____

_____

_____

_____

➤ After analysis of inventory issues, comment on any deficiencies noted, and
record recommendations for improvement:

_____

_____

_____

_____

_____

_____

_____

_____

Postage and Shipping

➤ Describe how the organization funds postage in the following areas:

Office postage meter: _____

_____

_____

Business reply mail: _____

_____

_____

Bulk mail: _____

_____

_____

Media mail: _____

_____

_____

Others: _____

_____

_____

➤ Has the organization communicated to the
post office that overages and refunds will be
credited to the organization's postal account   Yes   No   N/A
and that cash refunds are not permitted?   _____ _____ _____

If no, explain and record recommendations for improvement, if applicable:

_____

_____

_____

_____

_____

➤ Are policies and controls over access to
postage meters and accounts adequate   Yes   No   N/A
to ensure there is no unauthorized use?   _____ _____ _____

If no, explain and record recommendations for improvement, if applicable:

_____

_____

_____

_____

_____

➤ If the organization uses a shipping service, note the following:

Name of service _____

Account number _____

Address _____

_____

_____

Contact name _____

Telephone number _____

➤ Are the procedures surrounding utilization   Yes   No   N/A
of the organization's mail service adequate?   _____   _____   _____

If no, explain and record recommendations for improvement, if applicable:

_____

_____

_____

_____

_____

Comment on any specific issues that indicate that controls and policies surrounding postal meters, postal accounts, and shipping services are inadequate, and record recommendations for improvement:

_____

_____

_____

_____

_____

_____

_____

Travel Expenses

Objective: To ensure that the organization's travel expenses are reasonable and documented properly and that any income tax ramifications are handled properly. Describe the organization's existing travel policies and procedures, and make recommendations for improvement, if applicable:

➤ Does the organization issue travel advances?   Yes   No   N/A

                                                 _____ _____ _____

If yes, describe procedures:

_____

_____

_____

_____

_____

➤ Are travel expenses monitored to track
possible tax liabilities adequately (spouse   Yes   No   N/A
travel, company autos, entertainment, etc.)?   _____ _____ _____

If no, explain and make recommendations for improvement, if applicable:

_____

_____

_____

_____

_____

➤ Does the organization require original receipts   Yes   No   N/A
for travel expenses?   _____ _____ _____

If no, explain and record recommendations for improvement, if applicable:

_____

_____

_____

_____

_____

➤ Are travel expense policies current,   Yes   No   N/A
documented, and communicated properly?   _____ _____ _____

If no, explain and record recommendations for improvement, if applicable:

_____

_____

_____

_____

_____

➣ Does the organization use the per diem   Yes   No   N/A
method for meal allowances?   _____   _____   _____

If yes, describe procedures:

_____

_____

_____

_____

_____

➣ Does the organization monitor air fare
rates to ensure that it is benefitting from   Yes   No   N/A
the best available rates?   _____   _____   _____

If no, explain and record recommendations for improvement, if applicable:

_____

_____

_____

_____

_____

➣ Are the organization's travel expense
forms current, complete, and compliant   Yes   No   N/A
with the organization's travel policies?   _____   _____   _____

If no, explain and record recommendations for improvement, if applicable:

_____

_____

_____

_____

_____

Attach current travel approval and reimbursement forms.

Comment on any specific travel issues that indicate that controls and policies are not adequate, and record recommendations for improvement:

_____

_____

_____

_____

_____

Gift Offers

Objective: To ensure that all offers of gifts to employees by outside vendors, etc., are reported to the appropriate level of management for the purpose of assessing improper influence, ensuring that bribery is not taking place, etc.

➤ Does the organization have a policy requiring
all employees to make the appropriate level
of management aware that they have been
offered gifts by vendors, officials, etc.?

        Yes   No   N/A

        _____ _____ _____

If no, explain and record recommendations for improvement, if applicable:

_____

_____

_____

_____

_____

➤ Does the organization require all vendors
to report any intention of offering gifts to
employees to the appropriate level
of management?

        Yes   No   N/A

        _____ _____ _____

If no, explain and record recommendations for improvement, if applicable:

_____

_____

_____

_____

_____

Comment on any specific issues relating to gift offers that indicate controls are not adequate, and record recommendations for improvement:

_____

_____

_____

_____

_____

Information Technology

Objective: To document information technology (IT) organization and staffing, and assess competence.

➤ Title and name of IT director:

        Title   Name

_____   _____

➤ Titles and names of key IT staff:

        Title   Name

_____   _____

_____   _____

_____   _____

➤ Does the organization have formal job   Yes   No   N/A
  descriptions for all IT positions?   _____   _____   _____

  Comments:_____

  _____

  _____

  _____

  _____

➤ Do current IT staff have the proper
  education, background, and experience   Yes   No   N/A
  as relates to their duties?   _____   _____   _____

  Comments:_____

  _____

  _____

  _____

  _____

➤ Does it appear that the organization's
  current IT staffing is reasonable, considering Yes   No   N/A
  the current workload?   _____   _____   _____

Comments: _____

_____

_____

_____

_____

➤ Does the organization conduct adequate   Yes   No   N/A
   background checks for key IT staff?   ____   ____   ____

Comments: _____

_____

_____

_____

_____

➤ Are IT staff evaluated regularly?   Yes   No   N/A
                                                 ____   ____   ____

Comments: _____

_____

_____

_____

_____

➤ Is the segregation between IT and functions   Yes   No   N/A
   that it services adequate?   ____   ____   ____

Comments: _____

_____

_____

_____

_____

➤ Are IT personnel required to take   Yes   No   N/A
   annual vacations?   ____   ____   ____

Comments: _____

_____

_____

_____

_____

➤ Are IT personnel prohibited from initiating   Yes   No   N/A
transactions without appropriate approval?   ____   ____   ____

Comments:_____

_____

_____

_____

_____

➤ Is access to IT restricted to an "as needed"   Yes   No   N/A
   basis?   ____   ____   ____

Comments:_____

_____

_____

_____

_____

➤ Is the use of passwords effective?   Yes   No   N/A
   ____   ____   ____

Comments:_____

_____

_____

_____

_____

➤ Does the organization have written IT policies   Yes   No   N/A
and procedures, and are they adequate?   ____   ____   ____

Comments:_____

_____

_____

_____

_____

➤ Are IT staff included on the Fidelity Bond?   Yes   No   N/A

                                                                                 ____   ____   ____

Comments: _____

_____

_____

_____

_____

➤ Are IT files backed up effectively?   Yes   No   N/A

                                                                                 ____   ____   ____

Comments: _____

_____

_____

_____

_____

➤ Does the organization have a written   Yes   No   N/A
   disaster recovery plan, and is it adequate?   ____   ____   ____

Comments: _____

_____

_____

_____

_____

Fixed Assets

Objective: To ensure that purchases and disposals of fixed assets are properly authorized, carrying values are reasonable, and depreciation/amortization calculations are recorded accurately.

➤ Does the organization have a capital   Yes   No   N/A
acquisition budget?   _____   _____   _____

Comments:_____

_____

_____

_____

_____

➤ Does the organization use a purchase order   Yes   No   N/A
system for the acquisition of fixed assets? _____   _____   _____

Comments:_____

_____

_____

_____

_____

➤ What is the organization's capitalization cut-off point? $_____

➤ What depreciation method(s) does the organization use? _____

➤ Over what period of time does the organization depreciate different types of fixed assets?

Type of Asset	Depreciation Period
_____	_____
_____	_____
_____	_____
_____	_____
_____	_____

➤ Describe the organization's amortization policy(s):

_____

_____

_____

_____

_____

➤ Are fixed assets identified with serial numbers?   Yes   No

                                                    _____   _____

Comments: _____

_____

_____

_____

_____

➤ Has the existence of fixed assets acquired in   Yes   No   N/A
   the current year been verified?

                                          _____   _____   _____

Comments: _____

_____

_____

_____

_____

➤ Are fixed asset schedules current and accurate?   Yes   No   N/A

                                          _____   _____   _____

Comments: _____

_____

_____

_____

_____

➤ Do adequate controls exist with regard   Yes   No   N/A
   to safeguarding assets?

                                          _____   _____   _____

Comments:_____

_____

_____

_____

_____

➤ Document the organization's fixed assets retirement policy:

_____

_____

_____

_____

_____

➤ Are carrying values of fixed assets reasonable?   Yes   No   N/A

          _____   _____   _____

Comments:_____

_____

_____

_____

_____

➤ Are fixed assets adequately insured?   Yes   No   N/A

          _____   _____   _____

Comments:_____

_____

_____

_____

_____

After analysis of fixed asset policies and procedures, comment on any deficiencies noted and record recommendations for improvement:

_____

_____

_____

_____

_____

_____

_____

_____

_____

_____

_____

_____

_____

_____

_____

_____

_____

_____

_____

_____

_____

_____

_____

_____

_____

_____

_____

_____

_____

Investments

Objective: To ensure that investments are acquired properly, safeguarded, and valued properly.

➤ Does the organization have any investments on   Yes   No   N/A
its Balance Sheet/Statement of Financial Position?   _____   _____   _____

If the organization does have investments:

➤ Does the organization have an investment   Yes   No   N/A
acquisition policy?   _____   _____   _____

Comments:_____

_____

_____

_____

_____

➤ Briefly describe current investments:

_____

_____

_____

_____

_____

_____

➤ Who is responsible for investment security?

        Title(s)   Name(s)

_____   _____

_____   _____

_____   _____

_____   _____

_____   _____

➤ Are the individuals responsible for investment security bonded?

Yes _____ No _____ N/A _____

Comments: _____

_____

_____

_____

_____

➤ Are investments properly secured and protected?

Yes _____ No _____ N/A _____

Comments: _____

_____

_____

_____

_____

➤ Is access to investments on an "as needed" basis?

Yes _____ No _____ N/A _____

Comments: _____

_____

_____

_____

_____

➤ Are individuals with investment responsibilities required to take vacation?

Yes _____ No _____ N/A _____

Comments: _____

_____

_____

_____

_____

➤ Are investments monitored closely and valued currently?

        Yes   No   N/A

        ____   ____   ____

Comments:_____

_____

_____

_____

_____

➤ Are subsidiary investment records maintained accurately and compared to general ledger balances?

        Yes   No   N/A

        ____   ____   ____

Comments:_____

_____

_____

_____

_____

➤ Are interest income and/or dividend income monitored closely and accounted for properly?

        Yes   No   N/A

        ____   ____   ____

Comments:_____

_____

_____

_____

_____

After the analysis of investment issues has been completed, summarize material weaknesses noted and record recommendations for improvement:

_____

_____

_____

_____

_____

_____

_____

_____

_____

_____

_____

_____

_____

_____

_____

_____

_____

_____

_____

_____

_____

_____

_____

_____

_____

_____

_____

_____

_____

_____

_____

Prepaid Expenses, Deferred Income, Intangible Assets, etc.

Objective: To ensure that the above-referenced accounts are presented accurately in the financial statements.

➤ Does the organization have financial policies regarding recording expenditures as prepaid expenses?

Yes   No   N/A

_____   _____   _____

If yes, is the policy reasonable and applied accurately?

Yes   No

_____   _____

Comments:_____

_____

_____

_____

_____

If no, comment accordingly: _____

_____

_____

_____

_____

➤ Are subsidiary records accurate and reconciled to recorded amounts?

Yes   No   N/A

_____   _____   _____

Comments:_____

_____

_____

_____

_____

➤ Has the organization recorded intangible assets?   Yes   No

_____   _____

If yes, document specific intangible assets, accounting procedures, etc.:

_____

_____

_____

_____

_____

➤ Comment on any other accounts that require documentation:

_____

_____

_____

_____

_____

After review of prepared expenses, deferred income, intangible assets, etc., summarize any issues noted and record recommendations for improvement:

_____

_____

_____

_____

_____

_____

_____

_____

_____

_____

_____

_____

_____

_____

_____

_____

_____

_____

_____

Notes Payable/Long-Term Debt (Excluding Mortgages)

Objective: To ensure that liabilities are accurate and classified correctly, financing transactions are properly authorized, and interest expense is recognized properly.

➤ Does the organization have any long-term
debt financing arrangements with directors,   Yes   No
owners, key employees, etc.?   _____   _____

If yes, explain financing arrangements in detail, and note appropriate comments:

_____

_____

_____

_____

_____

➤ Is there an adequate segregation of
responsibilities among staff with regard
to approving financing arrangements,
recording financing arrangements,   Yes   No   N/A
preparing debt-service disbursements, etc.?   _____   _____   _____

Comments:_____

_____

_____

_____

_____

➤ Has interest expense recorded been verified   Yes   No   N/A
as accurate?   _____   _____   _____

If yes, comment on how verification was obtained from lending institutions, etc.:

_____

_____

_____

_____

_____

If no, comment accordingly:

_____

_____

_____

_____

_____

➤ Have principal balances recorded been   Yes   No   N/A
verified as accurate?   _____   _____   _____

If yes, comment on how verification was obtained from lending institutions, etc.:

_____

_____

_____

_____

_____

If no, comment accordingly:

_____

_____

_____

_____

_____

➤ Has the current portion of long-term debt   Yes   No   N/A
been accurately classified as a current liability? _____   _____   _____

Comments: _____

_____

_____

_____

_____

After review of notes payable and long-term debt, summarize any issues noted and record recommendations for improvement:

_____

_____

_____

_____

_____

_____

_____

_____

_____

_____

_____

_____

_____

_____

_____

_____

_____

_____

_____

_____

_____

_____

_____

_____

_____

_____

_____

_____

_____

Mortgages and Equity Lines of Credit

Objective: To ensure that mortgages are accurate and classified correctly, to evaluate if the current interest rate(s) is reasonable considering current economic conditions, and to investigate if equity lines of credit and so forth are classified and recorded correctly in the financial statements.

➤ Does the organization own any real property?   Yes   No

                                                                      _____   _____

If yes, describe property, acquisition date, and original cost:

Type of Property	Acquisition Date	Original Cost
_____	_____	_____
_____	_____	_____
_____	_____	_____
_____	_____	_____

➤ If there have been any capitalized improvements to real property, note improvement, improvement date, and cost:

Property	Improvement	Improvement Date	Cost
_____	_____	_____	_____
_____	_____	_____	_____
_____	_____	_____	_____

➤ Note information on *original* mortgage:

Property: _____

Mortgagee:_____

Amount of mortgage: $ _____

Interest rate: _____%

Length of mortgage:_____ years

Maturity date: _____

Debt service: $_____ month

➤ If the mortgage has been *refinanced,* note:

Property: _____

Mortgagee: _____

Refinanced amount: $ _____

Interest rate: _____ %

Length of mortgage: _____ years

Maturity date: _____

Debt service: $ _____ month

➤ If the organization should investigate
  refinancing the current mortgage, has this   Yes   No   N/A
  suggestion been offered to management?   _____   _____   _____

  Comments: _____

  _____

  _____

  _____

  _____

➤ Does the organization have an equity   Yes   No   N/A
  line of credit?   _____   _____   _____

  If yes, note details: _____

  _____

  _____

  _____

  _____

➤ What is the approximate market value of real property? $_____

➤ What is the approximate market value based on (commercial real estate
  appraisal, tax bill, comparable sale, etc.)?

  _____

  _____

  _____

_____

_____

➤ Is current insurance on real property reasonable? Yes   No   N/A

                                                                 _____   _____   _____

Comments: _____

_____

_____

_____

_____

After review of land and building detail, summarize any issues noted, and record recommendations for improvement:

_____

_____

_____

_____

_____

_____

_____

_____

_____

_____

_____

_____

_____

_____

_____

_____

_____

_____

_____

Payroll and Employee Fringe Benefits

Objective: To ensure that payroll and fringe benefit expenses are accurately recorded, that hirings and wage increases have been authorized properly, and that there are no "ghosts on the payroll."

Payroll

➤ Record titles and names of payroll-processing personnel:

Title   Name

_____   _____

_____   _____

_____   _____

_____   _____

➤ Are procedures for adding new employees   Yes   No
  to the payroll adequate?   ____   ____

Comments:_____

_____

_____

_____

_____

➤ Are a minimum of two people involved   Yes   No   N/A
  in adding new employees to the payroll?   ____   ____   ____

Comments:_____

_____

_____

_____

_____

➤ Are a minimum of two people involved
  in processing payroll, and are they required
  to sign their signatures attesting that payroll   Yes   No   N/A
  is accurate?   ____   ____   ____

Comments: _____

_____

_____

_____

_____

➤ Are two signatures required on all   Yes   No   N/A
  payroll checks?   _____   _____   _____

Comments: _____

_____

_____

_____

_____

➤ Are payroll checks signed by individuals   Yes   No   N/A
  not involved in processing payroll?   _____   _____   _____

Comments: _____

_____

_____

_____

_____

➤ If an outside payroll preparation service is   Yes   No   N/A
  used, are controls and reviews adequate?   _____   _____   _____

Comments: _____

_____

_____

_____

_____

➤ If a payroll service is used, note the following:

Name of Service _____

Address _____

_____

Contact Name _____

Telephone _____

➤ Is there a random check on payroll during
the year to ensure that wages are accurate
and there are no ghosts on the payroll?

        Yes   No

        _____   _____

Comments:_____

_____

_____

_____

_____

➤ Is there a random check on a federal tax
deposit during the year to ensure that it
is accurate?

        Yes   No

        _____   _____

Comments:_____

_____

_____

_____

_____

➤ Is there a random check on state or local
tax deposits during the year to ensure
that they are accurate?

        Yes   No   N/A

        _____   _____   _____

Comments:_____

_____

_____

_____

_____

➤ Is the payroll account reconciled promptly
at the end of each month by someone not
involved in processing payroll?

          Yes   No   N/A

Comments: _____

_____

_____

_____

_____

➤ Are payroll checks or direct deposit receipts
distributed to employees by employees not
involved in processing payroll?

          Yes   No   N/A

Comments: _____

_____

_____

_____

_____

➤ Does the organization use time sheets for
employees covered by the Fair Labor Standards
Act (FLSA), and are they signed by the
employee and approved by the employee's
direct supervisor?

          Yes   No   N/A

Comments: _____

_____

_____

_____

_____

➤ If payroll checks are issued, does anyone
monitor where they are being cashed?

          Yes   No

Note: Employees who do not deposit checks into bank accounts (expensive
check-cashing services, liquor stores, endorsing checks over to third parties,
etc.) may be ghosts or may have financial difficulties.

Comments:_____

_____

_____

_____

_____

➤ If employee loans or advances are
   permitted, are controls, procedures,   Yes   No   N/A
   and approvals adequate?   _____   _____   _____

   Comments:_____

   _____

   _____

   _____

   _____

➤ Are employee loans or advances balanced   Yes   No   N/A
   to the general ledger?   _____   _____   _____

   Comments:_____

   _____

   _____

   _____

   _____

➤ Are any employee loans unusually large, old,   Yes   No   N/A
   or unusual?   _____   _____   _____

   Comments:_____

   _____

   _____

   _____

   _____

➤ Do any employees have unusually large
   numbers of dependents listed on their   Yes   No
   W-4s, and are these validated as accurate?   _____   _____

Comments: _____

_____

_____

_____

_____

➤ Does the organization have a policy
  whereby payments for wages in cash   Yes   No   N/A
  is prohibited?   ____   ____   ____

Comments: _____

_____

_____

_____

_____

➤ Are policies monitored to ensure that
  payroll taxes are remitted on time to avoid   Yes   No   N/A
  penalties and interest for late payments?   ____   ____   ____

Comments: _____

_____

_____

_____

_____

➤ Are W-2s reviewed to ensure accuracy?   Yes   No   N/A
                                               ____   ____   ____

Comments: _____

_____

_____

_____

_____

➤ Are unemployment claims documents
  forwarded to someone not involved with
  payroll processing to ensure that the claims   Yes   No   N/A
  were initiated by a legitimate prior employee? ____   ____   ____

Comments:_____

_____

_____

_____

_____

After review of payroll procedures, summarize any issues noted, and record recommendations for improvement:

_____

_____

_____

_____

_____

_____

_____

_____

_____

_____

_____

_____

_____

_____

_____

_____

_____

_____

_____

_____

_____

_____

_____

Fringe Benefits

➢ Does the organization have an employee
fringe benefits program such as pension,
health insurance, paid leave, etc.?

	Yes	No	N/A
	_____	_____	_____

If yes, *briefly* summarize such benefits:

Pension, 401(k), etc.:_____

_____

_____

_____

Health insurance: _____

_____

_____

_____

Life insurance:_____

_____

_____

_____

Disability insurance: _____

_____

_____

_____

Other insurance: _____

_____

_____

_____

Cafeteria plan:_____

_____

_____

_____

Annual leave: _____

_____

_____

_____

Sick leave: _____

_____

_____

_____

Personal leave: _____

_____

_____

_____

Leave without pay: _____

_____

_____

_____

Other leave: _____

_____

_____

_____

Deferred compensation plans: _____

_____

_____

_____

Automobiles: _____

_____

_____

_____

Other employee fringe benefits not listed: _____

_____

_____

_____

_____

_____

_____

_____

_____

_____

_____

_____

_____

_____

_____

_____

➤ Are individuals responsible for employee
fringe benefit administration adequately   Yes   No   N/A
experienced and trained?   _____   _____   _____

Comments: _____

_____

_____

_____

_____

➤ Are W-2s reviewed to ensure that taxable   Yes   No   N/A
fringe benefits have been included?   _____   _____   _____

Comments: _____

_____

_____

_____

_____

➤ Are fringe benefit liabilities reconciled and
accurately recorded on the year-end financial
statement?

Yes	No	N/A
_____	_____	_____

Comments:_____

_____

_____

_____

_____

After review of employee fringe benefits, summarize any issues noted and record
recommendations for improvement:

_____

_____

_____

_____

_____

_____

_____

Equity/Net Assets

Objective: To ensure that all equity accounts are properly recorded and classified, agree with subsidiary records, and are in compliance with governing documents.

➤ List all equity/net assets currently listed on the Balance Sheet/Statement of Financial Position:

_____

_____

_____

_____

_____

➤ Is there an adequate segregation of responsibilities concerning equity transactions?

         Yes   No

Comments: _____

_____

_____

_____

➤ Are equity transactions in compliance with governing documents?

         Yes   No

Comments: _____

_____

_____

_____

➤ Are subsidiary records adequate, and do they reconcile with Balance Sheet/Statement of Financial Position amounts?

         Yes   No

Comments: _____

_____

_____

_____

After analysis of governing documents and equity policies and transactions, comment on any deficiencies noted and record recommendations for improvement:

_____

_____

_____

_____

_____

_____

_____

_____

_____

_____

_____

_____

_____

_____

_____

_____

_____

_____

_____

_____

_____

_____

_____

_____

_____

_____

_____

_____

_____

_____

Grants and Contracts (Not-for-Profit Organizations)

Objective: To ensure that grants and contracts are accounted for properly and that grant assets are adequately safeguarded.

➤ Does the organization have any grants
or contracts?

                                    Yes   No

If yes, briefly comment on the nature of the grants and contracts awarded, granting organizations, etc.:

_____

_____

_____

_____

_____

_____

➤ Is grant and contract accounting and financial
statement presentation adequate and in
accordance with Yellow Book and other related   Yes   No
requirements?

Comments: _____

_____

_____

_____

_____

➤ Are the safeguards surrounding grant and
contract assets adequate and in compliance   Yes   No
with related requirements?

Comments: _____

_____

_____

_____

_____

Comment on any grant or contract issues, and record recommendations for improvement:

_____

_____

_____

_____

_____

_____

_____

_____

_____

_____

_____

_____

_____

_____

_____

_____

_____

_____

_____

Restricted Fund Transactions (Not–for–Profit Organizations)

Objective: To ensure that restricted fund transactions are classified properly on the Statement of Financial Position and Statement of Activity, and that restricted assets are safeguarded properly.

➤ Does the organization have any temporarily   Yes   No
   restricted net assets?   _____   _____

➤ Briefly describe the nature of any temporarily restricted net assets:

_____

_____

_____

_____

_____

➤ Are temporarily restricted net assets
   classified properly on the Statement   Yes   No
   of Financial Position?   _____   _____

Comments: _____

_____

_____

_____

_____

➤ Are temporarily restricted net asset   Yes   No
   accounts adequately safeguarded?   _____   _____

Comments: _____

_____

_____

_____

_____

➤ Does the organization have any permanently   Yes   No
   restricted net assets?   _____   _____

➤ Briefly describe the nature of any permanently restricted net assets:

_____

_____

_____

_____

_____

➤ Are permanently restricted net assets
classified properly on the Statement of   Yes   No
Financial Position?   ____   ____

Comments:_____

_____

_____

_____

_____

➤ Are permanently restricted net assets   Yes   No
adequately safeguarded?   ____   ____

Comments:_____

_____

_____

_____

_____

Comment on any issues regarding the organization's restricted fund transactions,
and record recommendations for improvement:

_____

_____

_____

_____

_____

_____

Implementing an Embezzlement and Fraud Action Plan

Objective: To ensure that appropriate levels of management are informed as to what action to take in the event of embezzlement or fraud victimization.

➤ Has the CPA firm provided the
appropriate level of management with
an action plan of steps to take in the   Yes   No
event of fraud or embezzlement?   _____   _____

If no, explain and record recommendations for improvement, if applicable:

_____

_____

_____

_____

_____

➤ Have all employees signed the Conditions   Yes   No   N/A
of Employment agreement?   _____   _____   _____

If no, explain and record recommendations for improvement, if applicable:

_____

_____

_____

_____

_____

➤ Have all employees signed the Conflicts   Yes   No   N/A
of Interest agreement?   _____   _____   _____

If no, explain and record recommendations for improvement, if applicable:

_____

_____

_____

_____

_____

➤ Emergency Contact Information:

Chief Executive Officer:

    Name _____

    Home Address _____

    _____

    Home Telephone _____

    Cellular Telephone_____

    Business Telephone _____

Treasurer:

    Name _____

    Home Address _____

    _____

    Home Telephone _____

    Cellular Telephone_____

    Business Telephone _____

Chief Financial Officer:

    Name _____

    Home Address _____

    _____

    Home Telephone _____

    Cellular Telephone_____

    Business Telephone _____

Other Staff:

    Name _____

    Home Address _____

    _____

    Home Telephone _____

    Cellular Telephone_____

    Business Telephone _____

CPA Firm:

    Managing Partner Name _____

    Home Address _____

    _____

    Business Telephone _____

    Emergency Telephone _____

    Cellular Telephone _____

    In-Charge Accountant Name _____

    Home Address _____

    _____

    Business Telephone _____

    Emergency Telephone _____

    Cellular Telephone _____

Bank Contacts:

    Bank Officer Name _____

    Branch _____

    Branch Address _____

    _____

    Business Telephone _____

    Emergency Telephone _____

Insurance and Fidelity Bond:

    Insurance Agent Name _____

    Agency _____

    Address _____

    _____

    Business Telephone _____

    Emergency Telephone _____

    Policy Number _____

Attorney:

Name _____

Firm _____

Address _____

_____

Business Telephone _____

Emergency Telephone _____

Cellular Telephone_____

Police Information:

Station Name _____

Station Address _____

_____

Telephone Number to
Report Fraud or Embezzlement _____

➤ Have the appropriate levels of management been advised of the importance of
safeguarding original documents and   Yes   No
working from copies in the event of fraud?   _____   _____

If no, explain and record recommendations for improvement, if applicable:

_____

_____

_____

_____

_____

➤ Have the appropriate levels of management
been advised of the importance of taking
detailed and copious notes in the event of   Yes   No
fraud or embezzlement?   _____   _____

If no, explain and record recommendations for improvement, if applicable:

_____

_____

_____

_____

_____

➤ Are the appropriate levels of management aware
  of the importance of contacting the bank(s)
  immediately in the event of fraud or embezzle-   Yes   No
  ment, in order to have accounts, frozen?   _____   _____

If no, explain and record recommendations for improvement, if applicable:

_____

_____

_____

_____

_____

➤ Does the CPA firm have a predetermined
  fraud investigation team familiar with the   Yes   No   N/A
  specifics of the organization?   _____   _____   _____

If no, explain and record recommendations for improvement, if applicable:

_____

_____

_____

_____

_____

Comment on any specific embezzlement and fraud action plan issues that indicate
that more study and communication with management are needed:

_____

_____

_____

_____

_____

_____

Note any other internal control issues and recommendations for improvement not addressed in this guide:

_____

_____

_____

_____

_____

_____

_____

_____

_____

_____

_____

_____

_____

_____

_____

_____

_____

_____

_____

_____

_____

_____

_____

_____

_____

_____

_____

_____

_____

_____

_____

_____

_____

_____

_____

Internal Control Review Summary and Management Letter Issues

Objective: To summarize material internal control issues, communication of issues and recommendations for improvement to management, and potential Management Letter issues.

➤ Is the independent audit or internal
audit team satisfied that all issues
addressed in this book and the companion
website have been adequately reviewed
and that all recommendations for
improvement have been documented   Yes   No
properly in the work papers?   _____   _____

Comments: _____

_____

_____

_____

_____

➤ For each of the following areas, summarize *material* internal control deficiencies
noted, and record recommendations for improvement, where applicable:

   ➤ Finance and accounting staffing

   ➤ Internal Audit Committee

   ➤ Risk assessment and understanding the entity

   ➤ Brainstorming and employee interviews

   ➤ General internal control environment

   ➤ CPA financial statements, prior Management Letter issues, and consulting
       agreements

   ➤ Related party transactions

   ➤ Nepotism

   ➤ Conflicts of interest

   ➤ Accounting and financial policies and procedures manual

   ➤ Journal entries

   ➤ Management overrides

   ➤ Cash and cash equivalents

   ➤ Petty cash

   ➤ Receipts and accounts receivables

   ➤ Disbursements

   ➤ Accounts payable and other current liabilities

   ➤ Fidelity Bonds

➤ Bank and credit card statements

➤ Inventory

➤ Postage and shipping

➤ Travel

➤ Gifts

➤ Information technology

➤ Fixed assets

➤ Investments

➤ Prepaid expenses, deferred income, and intangible assets

➤ Notes payable and long-term debt

➤ Mortgages and equity lines of credit

➤ Payroll and employee fringe benefits

➤ Equity/net assets

➤ Grants and contracts

➤ Restricted fund transactions

➤ Fraud action plan

Comment on how material internal control weaknesses and recommendations for improvement have been adequately communicated to the appropriate level of management.

Management Letter Issues

Comment on any material internal control issues and recommendations for improvement that should be considered to be noted in the Management Letter:

Fraud Glossary[1]

Advance Fee Fraud. Falsely obtaining an advance fee for work or services not performed.

Alford **Plea.** Named after the Supreme Court case that upheld the practice under which a defendant pleads guilty, although continuing to assert innocence. Such a plea may be made to obtain the benefits of a plea agreement and to avoid potentially more dire consequences, such as the death penalty, if the defendant is convicted after trial.

Anti-Kickback Act of 1986. The provisions of this act are contained in Title 41, U.S. Code §§ 51–58. The act outlaws the giving or receiving of anything of value for the purpose of improperly obtaining or receiving favorable treatment in connection with U.S. government contracts.

Arbitration. Process whereby the dispute is submitted to an impartial third person who then decides the outcome of the case, that is, which party should win. The arbitrator acts as a judge or jury would, by deciding the case on its merits. An arbitration can be either "binding" or "nonbinding." If the arbitration is binding, then the decision of the arbitrator is final, and the parties cannot later submit their dispute to a judge or jury for determination.

Arraignment. Because of due process considerations, the defendant has to be brought before the court shortly after his arrest. He enters a plea at this time, in a

---

[1] © 1999 Association of Certified Fraud Examiners. Major portions of this Glossary reprinted with permission.

proceeding that is called an *arraignment*. He will be given notice of the charges against him, be informed of his rights, and, if applicable, bail will be set.

Attorney Work Product Doctrine. Under Rule 26(b)(3) of the Federal Rules of Civil Procedure, documents and tangible things that are prepared in anticipation of litigation or for a trial are protected by the work product privilege. The information may be disclosed only if the opposing party can show "substantial need" for the protected information and show that the information cannot be obtained from another source. The privilege extends to information prepared by or for a party or the party's representative, including attorneys and consultants.

Attorney-Client Privilege. This privilege precludes disclosure of communications between an attorney and client, but only if the following conditions are met: (1) the client retained the attorney, (2) to provide legal advice, (3) and thereafter communicated with the attorney on a confidential basis, and, (4) has not waived the privilege.

Audit Exceptions. Problems incurred during the course of an audit by the independent CPA or the IRS.

Best Evidence Rule. Prohibits a party from testifying about the contents of a document without producing the document itself. Also known as the *original writing rule*, it requires that when a witness testifies about the contents of a document, at least a fair copy of the original must be available for inspection. If there isn't an original, an authenticatible copy will do.

Bid-Rigging Schemes. The acceptance or payment of bribes or kickbacks in construction contracts. Bid-rigging schemes can be categorized based on the stage of bidding at which the fraudster exerts his influence. Bid-rigging schemes usually occur in the presolicitation phase, the solicitation phase, or the submission phase of the bidding process.

Billing Schemes. Type of asset misappropriation scheme that allows the perpetrator to misappropriate company funds without ever actually handling cash or checks while at work. There are three principal types of billing schemes: false invoicing via shell companies, false invoicing via nonaccomplice vendors, and personal purchases made with company funds.

Biological Theories. Biological theories maintain that criminal behavior is not the result of choice, that is, the calculation of benefits and potential losses, but rather is caused by the physical traits of those who commit crime.

***Brady* Material.**   Exculpatory information possessed by the government. Refers to the 1963 decision by the U.S. Supreme Court in *Brady v. Maryland*, 373 U.S. 83. Under *Brady*, the prosecution must disclose all evidence requested by the defendant that is material to guilt or punishment, that is, evidence that would tend to *exculpate* him or reduce his penalty. The government is expressly forbidden to conceal evidence that would call the charges into question.

Bribery.   Includes official bribery, which refers to the corruption of a public official, and commercial bribery, which refers to the corruption of a private individual to gain a commercial or business advantage. The elements of official bribery vary by jurisdiction, but generally are: (1) giving or receiving, (2) a thing of value, (3) to influence, (4) an official act.

Bustout.   A planned bankruptcy. It can take many different forms. The basic approach is for an apparently legitimate business to order large quantities of goods on credit, then dispose of those goods through legitimate or illegitimate channels. The perpetrators then close shop, absconding with the proceeds, and leaving the suppliers unpaid.

Cash Larceny.   The intentional taking away of an employer's cash (the term "cash" includes both currency and checks) without the consent and against the will of the employer.

Chain of Custody.   Refers to (1) who has had possession of an object, and (2) what they've done with it. The chain of custody must be preserved, or else the item cannot be used at trial.

Check Tampering.   Type of fraudulent disbursement scheme in which the perpetrator physically prepares the fraudulent check. Usually, the perpetrator takes physical control of a check and makes it payable to himself through one of several methods. Most check-tampering crimes fall into one of four categories: forged maker schemes, intercepted check schemes, concealed check schemes, and authorized maker schemes.

Chronemic Communication.   Refers to the use of time in interpersonal relationships to convey meaning, attitudes, and desires. If the respondent is late in keeping an appointment, for example, this might convey a lack of interest in or avoidance of the interview.

Churning.   Churning occurs when agents falsely tell customers that they can buy additional insurance for nothing by using built-up value in their current policies. In reality, the cost of the new policies frequently exceeds the value of the old ones.

Circumstantial Evidence.   Evidence that tends to prove or disprove facts in issue indirectly, by inference. Many fraud cases are proved entirely by circumstantial evidence, or by a combination of circumstantial and direct evidence, but seldom by direct evidence alone. The most difficult element to prove in many fraud cases—fraudulent intent—is usually proved circumstantially, and necessarily so, because direct proof of the defendant's state of mind, absent a confession or the testimony of a co-conspirator, is impossible.

Civil Monetary Penalty Law (CMPL).   The Civil Monetary Penalty Law (42 U.S. Code § 1320a-7a) was passed to impose administrative sanctions against providers who defraud any federally funded program by filing false claims by other improper billing practices. Any person (including an organization, agency, or other entity, but excluding a beneficiary) that presents or causes to be presented a claim for a medical or other item or service, when the person knows or should know the claim is false or fraudulent, is subject to a civil monetary penalty.

Common Law.   Consists of the usages and customs of a society as interpreted by the judiciary; it often is referred to as "judge-made" law.

Compensating Controls.   When adequate internal controls are precluded due to very small staffs or other factors, other controls are implemented.

Computer Crime.   Illegal act either conducted against the computer (such as data alteration) or in which the computer is an integral part of the improper act.

Computer Fraud.   Any defalcation or embezzlement accomplished by tampering with computer programs, data files, operations, equipment, or media, and result-ing in losses sustained by the organization whose computer system was manipu-lated. The distinguishing characteristic of computer fraud is that access occurs with the intent to execute a fraudulent scheme.

Computer Fraud and Abuse Act.   A statute enacted in 1984, Title 18 U.S. Code, Section 1030, makes certain computer-related activity a specific federal offense. In brief, Section 1030 punishes any intentional, unauthorized access to a "protected computer" for the purpose of: obtaining restricted data regarding national security, obtaining confidential financial information, using a computer that is intended for use by the U.S. government, committing a fraud, or damaging or destroying information contained in the computer.

Computer Hacking. Prior to newspapers using the term *hacker* to describe a computer criminal, the term was used to define a computer enthusiast. The term is now associated with unauthorized computer activity. Hacking or "phreaking" is basically the breaking into computers and telecommunications systems by learning the vulnerabilities of various types of hardware and software, and using a computer to systematically "guess" the telephone number, user's system identification, and password.

Computer Viruses. A computer virus is a program that contains instruction code to attack software. Some viruses are hidden computer programs that use all the computer's resources thereby shutting down the system or slowing it down significantly. Computer viruses range from the relatively harmless (displaying a message or greeting) to shutdowns of entire computer networks for extended periods.

Computer-Assisted Crime. Use of computers instead of other means to break the law.

Conflict of Interest. Occurs when an employee, manager, or executive has an undisclosed economic or personal interest in a transaction, which adversely affects that person's employer. As with other corruption frauds, conflict schemes involve the exertion of an employee's influence to the detriment of his company. In bribery schemes, fraudsters are paid to exercise their influence on behalf of a third party, whereas conflict cases involve self-dealing by an employee.

Corporate Fraud. Corporate fraud is any fraud perpetrated by, for, or against a business corporation. Corporate frauds can be internally generated (perpetrated by agents, employees, and executives of a corporation, for or against it, or against others) or externally generated (by others against the corporation, that is suppliers, vendors, customers).

COSO Report. The Committee of Sponsoring Organizations (COSO) was formed to support the implementation of the Treadway Commission findings. In 1992 the committee issued *Internal Control—Integrated Framework*. This report was a collaborative effort of the American Accounting Association, the American Institute of CPAs, the Financial Executives Institute, the Institute of Internal Auditors, and the Institute of Management Accountants.

Counterclaim.   A claim field by a defendant against the plaintiff in a civil suit. Popularly known as a "countersuit."

Criteria-Based Statement Analysis.   Analyzing the language used by the subject to assess its truthfulness.

Cross-Claim.   An action or claim between co-parties, that is, claims between two defendants or two plaintiffs.

Defalcation.   The act of a defaulter; act of embezzling; failure to meet an obligation; misappropriation of trust funds or money held in any fiduciary capacity; failure to properly account for such funds. Commonly applied to officers of corporations or public officials (*Black's Law Dictionary*, 1990).

Defamation.   The four elements of defamation are (1) a false statement of fact, (2) tending to subject the person to whom it referred to ill will or disrepute, (3) published to one or more persons, and (4) made without privilege.

Defense.   An assertion by a defendant in a criminal or civil suit that seeks to explain away guilt or civil liability for damages.

Demonstrative Evidence.   A tangible item that illustrates some material proposition (e.g., a map, a chart, a summary). It differs from real evidence in that demonstrative evidence was not part of the underlying event; it was created specifically for the trial. Its purpose is to provide a visual aid for the jury.

Deposition.   Sworn testimony given by a party or witness upon questioning by counsel for one of the parties before trial and outside of court, usually in a lawyer's office.

Diagnosis-Related Grouping (DRG).   A patient classification scheme that categorizes patients who are medically related with respect to primary and secondary diagnosis, age, and complications.

Direct Evidence.   Includes testimony or other evidence that tends to prove or disprove a fact in issue directly, such as eyewitness testimony or a confession. See also *Circumstantial Evidence*.

Discovery.   The formal process whereby the parties collect evidence and learn the details of the opposing case. Under federal rules, either party may take discovery regarding any matter, not privileged, that is relevant to the subject matter of the action, or that might lead to admissible evidence. The principal means of discovery are oral depositions, written interrogatories, and requests to produce documents.

Duty of Care.   The duty of a corporate officer, director, or high-level employee, as well as other people in a fiduciary relationship, to conduct business affairs prudently with the skill and attention normally exercised by people in similar positions.

Duty of Loyalty.   Requires that an employee/agent act solely in the best interest of the employer/principal, free of any self-dealing, conflicts of interest, or other abuse of the principal for personal advantage.

Duty of Obedience.   A standard requiring all members of the board of directors, officers, trustees, and key employees to follow federal and state laws as well as their organization's bylaws.

Economic Extortion.   Economic extortion cases are "Pay up or else. . ." corruption schemes—basically the flip side of bribery schemes. Instead of a vendor offering a payment to influence a decision, an employee demands that a vendor pay him to make a decision in that vendor's favor. If the vendor refuses to pay, he faces some harm such as a loss of business with the extorter's company.

Electronic Data Interchange.   Electronic Data Interchange (EDI) is the exchange of electronic data between computers, in which there is no human interaction.

Electronic Funds Transfer (EFT).   An electronic funds transfer (EFT) system is a network of operations designed to move instantaneously funds (e.g., deposits in savings and checking accounts and funds obtained through overdraft and credit arrangements) from one account or institution to another (*Bank Administration Manual*, Bank Administration Institute).

Embezzlement.   The wrongful appropriation of money or property by a person to whom it has been lawfully entrusted. Embezzlement implicitly involves a breach of trust, although it is not necessary to show a fiduciary relationship between the parties.

Employee Polygraph Protection Act.   Prohibits the use of polygraphs by most private employers unless the employer is engaged in an ongoing investigation involving economic loss or injury to the employer in the employer's business and has a reasonable suspicion that the employee is involved in the incident.

Encryption.   An encryption system consists of a cryptographic function, which scrambles an electronic transmission, and an inverse decrypt function, which restores the transmission to its original state. Encryption hardware and software can be used to scramble any communication by utilizing a complex mathematical formula. The only way to unscramble an encrypted message is to provide the unique answer "key," thus unlocking the message.

Evidence.   Anything perceivable by the five senses, and any proof such as testimony of witnesses, records, documents, facts, data, or tangible objects legally presented at trial to prove a contention and induce a belief in the minds of a jury.

Exclusionary Rule.   This rule commands that where evidence has been obtained in violation of the search and seizure protections guaranteed by the U.S. Constitution, the illegally obtained evidence cannot be used at the trial of the defendant. Under this rule, evidence that is obtained by an unreasonable search and seizure is excluded from admissibility under the Fourth Amendment, and this rule has been held to be applicable to the States. "Good faith exception" to the exclusionary rule provides that evidence is not to be suppressed under such rule where that evidence was discovered by officers acting in good faith and in reasonable, though mistaken, belief that they were authorized to take those actions. (*Black's Law Dictionary,* 1990.)

Expert Witness.   One who by reason of education or specialized experience possesses superior knowledge respecting a subject about which persons having no particular training are incapable of forming an accurate opinion or deducting a correct conclusion (*Kim Mfg., Inc. v. Superior Metal Treating, Inc.,* Mo. App., 537 S. W.2d 424, 428).

External Fraud Schemes.   Fraud schemes that are committed by outside organizations, typically by individuals or groups of individuals, against organizations.

Extortion.   The obtaining of property from another, with the other party's "consent" having been induced by wrongful use of actual or threatened force or fear. Fear might include the apprehension of possible economic damage or loss. A demand for a bribe or kickback also might constitute extortion.

Fair Credit Reporting Act.   One of the primary statutes limiting the access to personal information is the federal Fair Credit Reporting Act (FCRA). This statute regulates the dissemination of consumer information to third parties by consumer reporting agencies. It prohibits the disclosure of any consumer credit report (the terms are defined in the statute) except in accordance with the Act. Its purpose is to regulate the activities and record keeping of mercantile credit, insurance, and employment investigation agencies and bureaus.

False Claims and Statements.   Chapter 47 of Title 18, U.S. Code, contains a number of related provisions that punish false or fraudulent statements, oral or written, made to various federal agencies and departments. The principal statute is Section 1001, which prohibits such statements generally and overlaps with many of the more specific laws, such as Section 1014, that apply to false statements made on certain loan and credit applications.

False Imprisonment.   Restraint by one person of the physical liberty of another without consent or legal justification.

False Pretenses.   Illegally obtaining money, goods, or merchandise from another by fraud or misrepresentation. As a statutory crime, although defined in slightly different ways in the various jurisdictions, it consists generally of these elements: (1) an intent to defraud, (2) the use of false pretenses or representations regarding any existing facts, and (3) the accomplishment of the intended fraud by means of such false pretenses (*People v. Johnson*, 28 Mich. App. 10, 183 N.W.2d 813, 815, 816).

Fidelity Bond.   A policy issued by many large insurance companies under which the insured entity is covered against losses caused by the dishonest or fraudulent acts of its employees.

Financial Statement Fraud.   Fraud committed to falsify financial statements, usually committed by management, and normally involving overstating income or assets or understating liabilities or expenses.

Firewalls.   Firewalls are advanced software programs that effectively "lock up" access to an Internet site or email transmission. Firewalls are designed to control the interface between a network and the Internet. This technology surveys incoming and outgoing transmissions between the network and the Internet, stopping any questionable transmission attempt to access a sensitive area.

Foreign Corrupt Practices Act.   The provisions of the FCPA are found in Title 15, U.S. Code, §78m. The FCPA amended the 1934 Act to prohibit certain publicly held companies from making corrupt payments to foreign officials or political organizations. Other amendments to the Act make it illegal for any U.S. citizen to make such payments.

Forensic.   Of or relating to the courts.

Fraud.   Any intentional or deliberate act to deprive another of property or money by guile, deception, or other unfair means.

Fraud Examination.   A methodology for resolving fraud allegations from inception to disposition. More specifically, fraud examination involves obtaining evidence and taking statements, writing reports, testifying to findings, and assisting in the detection and prevention of fraud.

Fraud Theory Approach.   The fraud theory approach begins with the assumption, based on the known facts, of what might have occurred. Then that assumption is tested to determine whether it is provable. The fraud theory approach involves the following steps, in the order of their occurrence: (1) analyze available data, (2) create a hypothesis, (3) test the hypothesis, (4) refine and amend the hypothesis.

Fraudulent Disbursement Schemes.   Type of occupational fraud whereby an employee makes a distribution of company funds for a dishonest purpose. Examples of fraudulent disbursements include forging company checks, the submission of false invoices, doctoring timecards, and so forth.

Generally Accepted Accounting Principles (GAAP).   A technical term encompassing conventions, rules, and procedures governing acceptable accounting practice.

Generally Accepted Auditing Standards (GAAS).   Assumptions and rules that govern the CPA's ability to accept an auditing engagement and procedures that must be undertaken during the course of an audit.

Ghost Employee.   Refers to someone on the payroll who does not actually work for the victim company. Through the falsification of personnel or payroll records, a fraudster causes paychecks to be generated to a ghost. The fraudster or an accomplice then converts these paychecks. The ghost employee may be a fictitious person or a real individual who simply does not work for the victim employer. When the ghost is a real person, it is often a friend or relative of the perpetrator.

Ghost Vendor.   A process of billing an organization for goods or services that were never provided, by a vendor that does not exist. Usually perpetrated by someone with authority to approve invoices for payment.

Grand Jury.   Consists of 16 to 23 people sworn as jurors who meet in secret deliberation, usually in biweekly or monthly sessions, to hear witnesses and other evidence presented by prosecutors and to vote on indictments. An indictment or *true bill* must be concurred in by at least 12 jurors voting without the prosecutor present.

Horizontal Analysis.   A technique for analyzing the percentage change in individual financial statement items from one year to the next. The first period in the analysis is considered the base, and the changes to subsequent periods are computed as a percentage of the base period.

Illegal Gratuities.   Similar to bribery schemes, except that there is not necessarily an intent to influence a particular business decision before the fact. In the typical illegal gratuities scenario, a decision is made that happens to benefit a certain person or company. The party who benefitted from the decision then gives a gift to the person who made the decision. The gift could be anything of value. An illegal gratuity does not require proof of intent to influence.

Indictment.   In the federal system, all offenses punishable by death must be charged by indictment; all felonies (generally crimes punishable by imprisonment for a year or more) must be prosecuted by indictment, unless the defendant waives the requirement, in which case the prosecution may proceed by the filing of an "Information."

Information.   A charge signed only by the prosecutor, without the involvement of the grand jury. See also *Indictment*.

Insider Trading.   Consists of using nonpublic information relating to market securities trades.

Interrogatories.   Questions that are submitted to an opposing party in a lawsuit. Interrogatories cannot be given to anyone other than a party to a suit. Questions are submitted to the witness in writing. If no objection is given, then the party must answer the questions in writing. All answers must be sworn to under oath.

Interview.   A question-and-answer session designed to elicit information. It differs from an ordinary conversation in that the interview is structured, not free-form, and is designed for a purpose. An interview might consist of only one question or a series of questions.

Jencks Act.   The Jencks Act, 18 U.S. Code §3500, permits the defendant to obtain, prior to cross-examination, a government witness's prior statements (or portions thereof) that relate to the subject matter of his testimony on direct examination. However, the statute also protects statements from discovery until after the direct examination has been completed.

Jurisdiction.   Authority of a court to hear a particular type of case. A probate court, for instance, only has jurisdiction to hear cases related to wills and other probate matters. Lower trial courts (such as a justice of the peace court) may only have jurisdiction to hear matters under a certain dollar amount, for instance, cases with less than $5,000 in controversy.

Kickbacks.   In the commercial sense, refers to giving or receiving anything of value to influence a business decision without the employer's knowledge and consent.

Kinesic Interview.   Type of interview methodology that is different from traditional interview methods, because the interviewer is not necessarily looking for a confession from the interview subject. Instead of searching for information from the subject, the interviewer is attempting to assess whether the subject is telling the truth. In the book *The Kinesic Interview Technique,* authors Frederick C. Link and D. Glen Foster define the kinesic interview technique as "[An interview technique] used for gaining information from an individual who is not willingly or intentionally disclosing it."

Kinetic Communication.   Involves the use of body movement to convey meaning. For example, a person who feels shame normally will drop the eyes to avoid the glance of another. This is not only to avoid seeing disapproval, but to conceal personal shame and confusion.

Kiting.   The wrongful practice of taking advantage of the float, the time that elapses between the deposit of a check in one bank and its collection at another. The drawer uses funds that are not his by drawing checks against deposits that have not yet cleared through the banks. Kiting consists of writing checks against a bank account where funds are insufficient to cover them, hoping that before they are presented, the necessary funds will be deposited (*Black's Law Dictionary,* 1990).

Land Flip.   Practice of buying and selling real estate very quickly, often several times a day, or at least within a few months. With each sale the price is increased. The sales often are transacted between related parties or with shell corporations.

Their sole purpose is to increase the selling price. Ultimately, the price becomes insupportable.

Larceny.   The wrongful taking of money or property of another with the intent to convert it or to deprive the owner of its possession and use. The transaction has already been recorded and is "on the books."

Libel.   Form of defamation whereby the offending material is communicated by writing or pictures, as opposed to purely oral means.

Management Letter.   Written communication from the auditing CPA firm to the client, detailing material issues that have come to the attention of the auditor during the course of the audit. The Management Letter is not included with audited financial statements and is not limited to internal control issues.

Mail Fraud.   The federal mail fraud statute is Title 18, U.S. Code, §1341. The gist of the offense is the use of the mails as an integral part of a scheme to defraud. The mailing itself does not need to contain the false and fraudulent representations, as long as it is an integral part of the scheme. What is integral or incidental depends on the facts of each case; generally, a mailing that helps advance the scheme in any significant way will be considered sufficient.

Material Weakness.   Weaknesses in internal control that would probably not be detected by auditors, internal auditors, or employees in a timely manner.

Mediation.   Process whereby an impartial third person assists the parties in reaching a resolution of the dispute. The mediator does not decide who should win, but instead works with the parties to reach a mutually agreeable settlement.

***Miranda* Rights.**   Refers to the Supreme Court ruling in the landmark case of *Miranda v. Arizona*, 348 U.S. 436 (1966), that the police must give the following warnings before interrogating any suspect held in custody: (1) the suspect has the right to remain silent, (2) any statements can be used against him at trial, (3) the suspect has a right to the assistance of an attorney, and (4) an attorney will be appointed to represent the suspect if he cannot afford to retain one.

Misapplication.   Wrongful taking or conversion of another's property for the benefit of someone else.

Misappropriation.   The unauthorized, improper, or unlawful use of funds or other property for a purpose other than that for which it was intended.

Misrepresentation of Material Facts.   The deliberate making of false statements to induce the intended victim to part with money or property. The elements normally include: (1) a material false statement, (2) knowledge of its falsity, (3) reliance on the false statement by the victim, and (4) damages suffered.

Money Laundering.   The disguising of the existence, nature, source, ownership, location, and disposition of property derived from criminal activity. The "washing" of money includes all forms of illegal activities. In most instances, the goal is to conduct transactions in cash (currency) in such a way as to conceal the true nature of transactions.

Multilevel Marketing (MLM).   Use of individual sellers and a graduated payment scale to move products. Illegal MLMs use the product as a front while basing their return on new people recruited into the plan.

Net Worth.   The amount by which assets exceed liabilities.

Noncompetition Agreement.   An agreement whereby an employee agrees not to work for competing companies within a certain period of time after leaving a company.

Nondisclosure Agreement.   A written agreement that provides that all proprietary, confidential, or trade secret information learned by the party in the course of business dealings must be kept confidential and must not be disclosed to any third parties.

Norming.   Sometimes referred to as "calibrating," norming is the process of observing behavior before critical questions are asked, as opposed to doing so during questioning. People with truthful attitudes will answer questions one way; those with untruthful attitudes generally will answer them differently.

Occupational Fraud and Abuse.   The use of one's occupation for personal enrichment through the deliberate misuse or misapplication of the employing organization's resources or assets. Simply stated, occupational frauds are those in which an employee, manager, officer, or owner of an organization commits fraud to the detriment of that organization. The three major types of occupational fraud are: corruption, asset misappropriation, and fraudulent statements (which include financial statement schemes).

Off-Book Fraud. Involves vendor and vendor employees engaging in bribes, scams, kickbacks, conflicts of interest, bribery, and corruption. Detected by means of tips or complaints from sources either inside or outside the company.

On-Book Fraud. Involves employees manipulating accounting records. Detected by means of basic audit tests in high-risk areas, using original source documents.

Oversight Committee. An oversight committee should be established to review uniformity in decision making. Further, it should act as a tribunal for the presentation of additional information *to change* or assist management in making appropriate decisions regarding fraud investigations.

Paralinguistic Communication. Involves the use of volume, pitch, and voice quality to convey meaning. One of the basic differences between written and verbal communication is that oral speech gives the full range of nonverbal accompaniment. For example, a "no" answer might not really mean no; it depends on the way in which the "no" is said.

Parole Evidence. Oral or verbal evidence; that which is given by word of mouth, the ordinary kind of evidence given by witnesses in court (*Black's Law Dictionary*, 1990).

Parole Evidence Rule. This evidence rule seeks to preserve the integrity of written agreements by refusing to permit contracting parties to attempt to alter the import of their contract through use of contemporaneous oral declarations (*Black's Law Dictionary*, 1990).

Phishing. An email scheme whereby a fraudster poses as a legitimate enterprise to gather financial information such as credit card and bank account numbers from an unknowing victim.

Ponzi Scheme. The term *Ponzi* refers to illegal operations that use financial instruments of some sort to extract money from victims; there are few or no actual investments being made, just funds passing up a ladder.

Privacy Act of 1974. Restricts information about individuals, both employees and nonemployees, that might be gathered by *government agencies*. This information might include a person's education, finances, medical history, criminal history, employment history, and identifying information (fingerprint, voice print, or photograph). The employee might have access to the information unless it is investigatory material compiled for law enforcement purposes, statistical records, or material compiled solely for determining suitability, eligibility, or qualification for federal service or promotion.

Probable Cause. Reasonable cause; having more evidence for than against. A reasonable ground for belief in certain alleged facts. A set of probabilities that is grounded in the factual and practical considerations that govern the decisions of reasonable and prudent persons and is more than mere suspicion but less than the quantum of evidence required for conviction (*Black's Law Dictionary*, 1990).

Proxemic Communication. Use of interpersonal space to convey meaning. The relationship between the interviewer and respondent is both a cause and effect of proxemic behavior. If the distance between the interviewer and the respondent is greater, there is more of a tendency for them to watch each other's eyes for clues to meaning.

Psychological Theories. Refers to theories of behavior rooted in psychology and based on the view that criminal behavior is the product of mental processes.

Pyramid Scheme. A scheme in which a buyer or participant is promised a payment for each additional buyer or participant recruited by that person.

Qui Tam Suit. A *qui tam* suit is one in which a private individual sues on behalf of the government to recover damages for criminal or fraudulent actions committed against the government. It is a civil, not a criminal, suit. Most qui tam actions are brought under the False Claims Act, 31 U. S. Code §3729 et seq.

Racketeer Influenced and Corrupt Organizations Act (RICO). Title 18, U.S. Code, §1961, et. seq. The statute outlaws the investment of ill-gotten gains in another business enterprise, the acquisition of an interest in an enterprise through certain illegal acts, and the conduct of the affairs of an enterprise through such acts. Criminal penalties include stiff fines and prison terms, as well as the forfeiture of all illegal proceeds or interests. Civil remedies include treble damages, attorney fees, dissolution of the offending enterprise, and other penalties.

Ratio Analysis. A means of measuring the relationship between two different financial statement amounts. The relationship and comparison are the keys to the analysis.

Real Evidence. Refers to physical objects that may be introduced as evidence at a legal proceeding. A canceled check, an invoice, a ledger, letters, and documents are real evidence, but the term includes any physical evidence.

Relevant Evidence. Rule 401 of the Federal Rules of Evidence defines *relevant evidence* as evidence "having any tendency to make the existence of any fact that is of consequence to determination of the action more probable or less probable than it would be without the evidence." In other words, relevant evidence is evidence that tends to prove or disprove a fact in issue.

Reportable Condition. A significant deficiency in internal controls that could lead to fraud if not corrected.

Routine Activities Theory. A variation of classical theory, this theory holds that both the motivation to commit crime and the supply of offenders are constant. There always will be a certain number of people motivated by greed, lust, and other forces inclining toward lawbreaking.

Search Warrants. Issued by a judge upon presentation of probable cause to believe that records or other items are being used or have been used in the commission of a crime. An affidavit usually is used to support the request for the search warrant. The affidavit must describe in detail the reason(s) the warrant is requested, along with the place the evidence is thought to be kept. Courts cannot issue search warrants without sufficient cause; the Fourth Amendment to the Constitution protects individuals against unreasonable searches and seizures.

Sentencing Guidelines. The Sentencing Reform Act of 1984 provided for the development of guidelines for the sentencing of individual and organizational offenders. The individual guidelines became effective in 1987, and the guidelines for organizations in 1991.

Shell Companies. Fictitious business entities created for the sole purpose of committing fraud. They may be nothing more than a fabricated name and a post office box that an employee uses to collect disbursements from false billings.

Skimming. Removal of cash from a victim entity prior to its entry in an accounting system. Employees who skim from their companies steal sales or receivables before they are recorded in the company books. Skimming schemes are known as "off-book" frauds, meaning money is stolen before it is recorded in the victim organization's accounts.

Slander. Form of defamation whereby a person, persons, or organization is offended by oral rather than written means.

Sliding. "Sliding" is the term used for including additional coverages in the insurance policy without the knowledge of the insured. The extra charges are hidden in the total premium, and because the insured is unaware of the coverage, few claims are ever filed. For example, motor club memberships, accidental death, and travel accident coverages can usually be slipped into the policy without the knowledge of the insured.

Social Control Theory. Travis Hirschi, in his 1969 book, *Causes of Delinquency,* first articulated the *social control theory.* Essentially, control theory argues that the institutions of the social system train and press those with whom they are in contact into patterns of conformity. The theory rests on the thesis that to the extent a person fails to become attached to the variety of control agencies of the society, his/her chances of violating the law are increased.

Social Learning Theories. These theories hold that criminal behavior is a function of the way people absorb information, viewpoints, and motivations from others, most notably from those to whom they are close, such as members of their peer group. Social learning theorists believe that all people have the potential to commit crime if they are exposed to certain kinds of circumstances.

Social Process Theories. These theories hold that criminality is a function of individual socialization and the social-psychological interactions people have with the various organizations, institutions, and processes of society. Although they differ in many respects, the various social process theories all share one basic concept: All people regardless of their race, class, or gender, have the potential to become delinquents or criminals.

Social Structure Theories. Theories of criminology that concentrate on the kinds of societies that generate particular levels of crime. For example, why is crime so low in Japan and so high in the United States? Such theorists argue that people living in equivalent social environments seem to behave in a similar, predictable fashion.

Subpoena Duces Tecum. A legal order requiring the production of documents.

Suspicious Activity Reports. Effective April 1, 1996, the Office of the Comptroller of the Currency (OCC) requires national banks to submit a Suspicious Activity Report (SAR) under certain circumstances (12 C.F.R. §21.11, as amended). Reports are required if there is a known or suspected criminal violation committed against the bank or involving a transaction conducted through the bank.

Tax Fraud. "the actual intentional wrongdoing, and the intent required . . . to evade a tax believed to be owing." Fraud implies bad faith, intentional wrongdoing, and a sinister motive. It is never imputed or presumed and the courts will not sustain findings of fraud upon circumstances which at most create only suspicion. See 14 Mertens, *Law of Federal Income Taxation*, sec. 55.21, page 64 (1991 Rev); *Ross Glove Co. v. Commissioner*, 60 TC 569 (1973).

Telemarketing Fraud. Used to refer to fraud schemes that are perpetrated over the telephone; they most often consist of calls by the telemarketer to the victim to deceive the victim into purchasing goods or services.

Trade Secret. Includes secret formulas and processes, but also any other proprietary information, such as customer and price lists, sales figures, business plans, or any other confidential information that has a value to the business and would be potentially harmful if disclosed.

Treadway Commission. The National Commission on Fraudulent Financial Reporting (commonly known as the Treadway Commission) was established in 1987 with the purpose of defining the responsibility of the auditor in preventing and detecting fraud. The commission was formed by the major professional auditing organizations: the American Institute of Certified Public Accountants, the Institute of Internal Auditors, and the National Association of Accountants.

Trespass. The unauthorized, intentional, or negligent entry upon the property of others. A claim of trespass might arise from a search of an employee's locker. It is particularly applicable to surveillance at an employee's home.

Twisting. Twisting is the replacement, usually by high-pressure sales techniques, of existing policies for new ones. The primary reason, of course, is for the agent to profit, because first-year sales commissions are much higher than commissions for existing policies.

Uniform Commercial Code Filings. In order to obtain a perfected security interest in personal property, a lender must file a Uniform Commercial Code (UCC) statement with the secretary of state or the county. Banks, finance companies, and other lenders will generate records or recorded filings of financial transactions conducted with individuals and businesses, such as purchases of household furniture, appliances, boats and yachts, automobiles, aircraft, and business equipment.

Uniform Crime Reports.   The Federal Bureau of Investigation (FBI) compiles statistics on the extent of crime in the United States in a document called the *Uniform Crime Report* (UCR). The report is put together on the basis of information voluntarily submitted by more than 15,000 law enforcement departments. This includes virtually every significant public policing agency in the country.

Venue.   The geographical area covered by the court. A trial court in Dallas County, Texas, for example, can only hear cases that have some connection with either parties or events that occurred in that county. Venue is technically an element of the court's jurisdiction.

Vertical Analysis.   A technique for analyzing the relationships between the items on an income statement, balance sheet, or statement of cash flows by expressing components as percentages.

Whistleblowers.   Employees who report illegal or unethical conduct of their employers. Federal law and many state laws provide, in some instances, protection to employees who report improper or illegal acts to government authorities. Most of these laws protect the employee from any adverse employment action or retaliatory action from the employer.

Wire Fraud.   The federal wire fraud statute is Title 18, U.S. Code, § 1343. It prohibits transmission "by means of wire, radio, or television communication in interstate or foreign commerce, any writings, signs, signals, pictures, or sounds for the purpose of executing such scheme or artifice." The wire fraud statute often is used in tandem with mail fraud counts in federal prosecutions. Unlike mail fraud, however, wire fraud requires an interstate or foreign communication for a violation.

Yellow Book Standards.   Standards for audits of government organizations, programs, activities, and functions, and of government assistance received by contractors, nonprofit organizations, and other nongovernment organizations, developed by the Comptroller General of the United States, General Accounting Office (GAO). These standards are by and large taken from Generally Accepted Accounting Principles. However, *Government Auditing Standards*, also known as the *Yellow Book*, goes beyond the AICPA standards. Generally Accepted Government Auditing Standards (GAGAS) are to be followed by auditors and audit organizations when required by law, regulation, agreement, contract, or policy.

Index